CYCLING

CYCLING

Ruth Marr

Fifth House
PUBLISHERS
Saskatoon Saskatchewan

Credits
Designed, typeset and illustrated by Robert MacDonald, MediaClones Inc.,
Toronto, Saskatoon and Winnipeg
Cover photo and separation courtesy of Norco Products Ltd.
Vancouver, Winnipeg and Toronto
Text photos by Ruth Marr, except those on page 39 by
Robert Bisson and page 149 by Jim Wilkie.
The photos on pages 11 and 87 are courtesy of Travel Manitoba

Canadian Cataloguing in Publication Data

Marr, Ruth 1958-
Manitoba Outdoor Adventure Guide: Cycling
ISBN 0-920079-50-4

1. Bicycle touring — Manitoba. 2. Cycling paths — Manitoba.
3. Manitoba — Description and travel — 1981- I. Title

GV1046.C32M37 1989 796.6'097127 C89-098044-6

Published by
Fifth House Publishers
Suite One, 128 2nd Avenue North
Saskatoon Saskatchewan S7K 2B2
Canada

Printed in Canada

Table of Contents

Acknowledgements

Thank you most of all to Rick and Marlene, who are both wonderful cycling companions, and were constant in their support and enthusiasm.

Special thanks to Bob Fenton of the Winnipeg Cycletouring Club, Ken Schykulski, and Paul Kruger for information, review and encouragement; to the Galbraiths of Swan River Valley, Ruth DeJong of Snow Valley and Doug Keith of Birch for permission to share their land with cyclists; and to Manitoba Parks Branch and others for permission to include trails crossing Crown land.

Thank you to the many others who contributed suggestions, comments, information, and photographs including: Wayne Antichow, Andrea Auch, Larry Bidlake, Robert Bisson, Bruce Bremner, Dan Bulloch, Brendan Carruthers, Jim Crone, Don Dunnigan, Greg Gunthar, Laurie Penton, Carl and Shirley Leslie, Ken Sauerbrei, Travel Manitoba, and Jim Wilkie.

To Rick

INTRODUCTION

Grab a bike, crank the pedals and discover the fun and adventure of cycling in Manitoba. This is a book about the variety of rides in this province, and it is intended for both residents and visitors, and for all levels of cyclists, from families and recreational cyclists to hill-hungry racers.

The emphasis of the book is on choice in the outdoors of Manitoba. Detailed descriptions and maps carry you down paved and gravel roads, and up trails and back roads in parks and forests. Some rides are short and easy, others long and tough or technically demanding. Look for day rides near your home, or plan a tour from two to 12 days long. What the book does not offer are detailed routes for riding inside the towns and cities of Manitoba: use this book for adventures beyond those boundaries.

The entire province is represented in over 70 routes. Consider the suggestions for additional rides to discover further kilometers of pedaling in Manitoba. As comprehensive as this listing is, there are more roads and trails to be explored and enjoyed. Suggestions or comments regarding new or existing routes in the province are welcomed for future editions of the book. Please address these to the author, care of the publisher.

How to Use this Book

The categories of cycling in Manitoba described in this book are termed paved road, gravel road, and off road riding. Paved road is self-explanatory. Gravel road refers to unpaved roads, and most of those in this book are numbered Provincial Roads. Some are roads maintained by rural municipalities. Off road riding, as defined in this book, includes back roads and trails in provincial parks, forests and wildlife management areas.

Cycling routes are arranged alphabetically within each of the three main sections of the book, which are titled Paved Road, Gravel Road and Off Road. To select a cycling route, flip through the descriptions, or refer to the summary maps and tables at the beginning of each section. The maps show the general location of all paved, gravel, and off road routes in the book. Use the summary tables to select routes based on geographical location or level of difficulty.

The route descriptions are structured similarly for all three categories of cycling. A main title describes a route or a cycling area, and there may be several possible routes under that main title. Introductory paragraphs give you a feel for cycling in the area. A map is provided, its scale dependent on the type of cycling distances covered. For each route, several titled paragraphs provide explicit information on:

Type: the category of the ride, whether day rides or tours are possible; and for off road riding, whether the riding surface is a trail or a back road.

Access: directions to the start and end of routes. Parking is noted if appropriate.

Facilities: camping, accommodation, stores, restaurants, washrooms or latrines along or near the route. Note that no specific names or recommendations are provided. Refer to the Accommodations Guide prepared by Travel Manitoba (see 'Getting Further Information' p.17). Water is considered available at the above facilities (except latrines), but special sources are also noted.

Distances: of the single route, or of several options within a system of trails. Distances may be approximate for off road routes. Suggested daily distances are provided for tours. Cycling times are not estimated, as they are extremely variable. Experience is your best guide: try a few of the routes here when you have ample time, and get a feel for your riding speed for different distances and over different surfaces.

Difficulty: a rough rating system of easy, moderate and difficult has been applied to all the trails using criteria of distance, topography, and riding surface. The key reason for a route's designated difficulty is provided with the rating. A range of difficulty levels may be rated for one route, indicating that short and easy routes can be selected, or extra kilometers or hills added. These variations are noted in the text.

For each route, one or more ride is explained in detail. One direction of travel is described, with turning instructions provided as both compass directions and as left or right turns. Follow the directions carefully, or devise your own approach to the route. In some cases suggestions are made for further exploration in the area. Read, plan, then set out to ride and enjoy.

Three abbreviations used throughout the book are: PTH - Provincial Trunk Highway, usually a paved main highway; PR - Provincial Road, a paved or gravel secondary highway; B&B - Bed and Breakfast accommodation.

Welcome to Manitoba

Manitoba is Canada's 'keystone' province, set in the heart of the country. Although it represents only 6.5% of Canada's area, Manitoba sprawls over 650,000 square kilometers. Within these boundaries is a wide diversity of landscapes and ecosystems. The variety and beauty of Manitoba are among its assets as a province for cycling.

Landforms

The four main physiographic regions of Manitoba have been strongly shaped by the glacial period. In the far north is the Hudson Bay Lowland, beyond roads and the reach of bicycles. The Precambrian Shield is the largest physiographic region, beginning in Whiteshell Provincial Park in the southeast, and cutting across eastern and northern Manitoba. Very few of the cycling routes in this book cross the rocks of the Shield.

The Manitoba Lowlands are responsible for Manitoba's flat reputation. This is rich farmland, derived from the clays of glacial Lake Agassiz, and centered around the Red River Valley. Over one sixth of the province is fresh water, including the three large lakes plunked in the center of these lowlands (Lakes Winnipeg, Winnipegosis, and Manitoba). Sand deposits from the glacial period provide some topographic relief in the Manitoba Lowlands, especially east of the Red River in a region now cloaked by provincial forests, and further west in the extensive sand dunes of the Carberry region.

Cyclists can find plenty of hills in the fourth physiographic region, the Southwestern Uplands. The rise of the Manitoba Escarpment, slicing northwest through the province, announces this region. The escarpment has been cut by past and present rivers, carving distinctive uplands, including the Pembina Hills and Riding, Duck and Porcupine Mountains. Once on the uplands, bedrock geology, glacial deposits and river valleys combine into a diversity of hills, including precipitous drops, gently rolling farmland, and hummocky forestlands with constant ascents and descents.

Vegetation and Wildlife

Manitoba's vegetation reflects the general physiographic regions and responds to local influences such as climate, soils, and topography. Cyclists will not see the tundra around the Hudson Bay, although northern cycling routes cross boreal or coniferous forests. Mixed deciduous-coniferous, deciduous forests and aspen parkland (aspen groves mixed with grasslands or fields), ring many of the routes described in this book. In southwestern and central Manitoba, cycle past rare remnant tall-grass and mixed-grass prairie among the croplands.

Wildlife viewing is an asset to cycling in Manitoba, especially in the more remote and less populated areas. Riding Mountain National Park excels in this regard, with elk, moose, deer, bear, and numerous furbearers and rodents among its resident species. Watch for white-tailed deer, coyotes, foxes and rabbits along the roads of southern Manitoba.

Climate

Manitoba's continental climate has benefits and disadvantages for cyclists. The long and cold winters preclude cycling for all but the hardiest enthusiasts. When summer suddenly appears it can be wonderful, with warm, sunny weather prevailing. Average monthly weather data for Winnipeg are:

	APR	MAY	JUNE	JULY	AUG	SEPT	OCT
A.MAX.TEMP.	8.9	18.0	23.1	25.	2	11.5	
A.MIN.TEMP	2.2	4.5	10.5	13.3	11.8	6.3	0.7
DAILY TEMP.	3.4	11.3	16.8	19.6	18.	12.4	6.1
EX.MAX.TEMP.	34.3	37.0	36	37.8	40.	36.2	29.4
EX.MIN.TEMP.	-26.3	-11.	-3.	-17.2			
PRECIP.DAYS	8	10	11	11	11	11	8
A.PRECIP.(mm)	38.5	65.7	80.1	775.2	53.3	30.9	

(A.=AVERAGE; D.=DAILY; MAX.=MAXIMUM; MIN.=MINIMUM;
TEMP.=TEMPERATURE IN DEGREES CELSIUS; EX.=EXTREME; PRECIP.
=PRECIPITATION)

Average temperatures for Winnipeg are slightly higher than those experienced in the rest of the province. Southwestern Manitoba receives less precipitation on fewer days, while higher elevations, such as Riding Mountain, tend to receive higher rainfall or snow over approximately the same number of days.

Wind is an important consideration, especially for highway riding. In the Red River Valley southern winds prevail throughout the cycling months. When the wind does blow from the north, it is usually very strong. Winnipeg has the dubious distinction of being the windiest recording station in the province. In western Manitoba, easterly and westerly winds prevail from April to October, although northern winds are strong in April and May. In northern Manitoba (The Pas), winds tend to blow from the southeast and the west, although calm conditions are frequent in July and August. Throughout the province, winds are strongest in April and May.

Population

Most of Manitoba's one million residents are clustered in the southern third of the province, concentrated around the Red River. Winnipeg is the largest city, housing 60% of the provincial population. Other cities or major towns across the province include Selkirk, Portage la Prairie, Brandon, Dauphin, The Pas, Flin Flon and Thompson. The province is proud of its broad ethnic background, including people of native, French, English, Metis, Ukrainian and Mennonite origins.

Getting to Manitoba

In the center of Canada, Manitoba is accessible by road (especially by the Trans-Canada Highway running east to west across the country), by plane from neighboring provinces and states, by train and by bus. American citizens require proof of citizenship to cross the border into Manitoba.

Getting Started

To start cycling in Manitoba, you need a bike and the ability to ride it. After those essentials, all levels of detail and finesse can be added, starting with the type and quality of the bicycle, the range of items which might adorn the bicycle, and the level and extent of your cycling skills and interest. A vast array of books have discussed virtually every aspect of bicycles and cycling, and this section does not intend to duplicate the effort. A few points to get you out on your way to the roads and trails of Manitoba are highlighted, but the emphasis is on sources of more information. Specific pointers are also offered in the introductions to the Paved Road, Gravel Road and Off Road sections.

Books are one source of information, and several are recommended. Check in your local libraries and bookstores for other titles. Although favoring touring, Bikecentennial in the United States has a thorough mail order listing of bike books, while the mail order bike stores in Canada (Bloorcycle in Toronto and Ridley's in Calgary) also list books. Cycling magazines are an excellent source of current information on every cycling topic. Search out other cyclists through bicycle shops or organizations (see 'Getting Involved') for 'hands on' and local information. Most of all, ride, experiment, and gain experience and enjoyment.

Buying a Bicycle

Buying a bicycle in Manitoba is not much different from buying a bicycle elsewhere. A successful bike purchase depends on finding the type of bicycle that suits you, and an individual bicycle that fits you. Scan the route descriptions in this book to get a feel for the type of riding that appeals to you in Manitoba, then throw in your biases, dreams, and budget to decide which bike is best for you. Any bike is enjoyable on paved roads. Sturdy touring road bikes or mountain bikes can handle the routes described in the Gravel Road section. The same applies for the back roads in the Off Road section. Mountain bikes are recommended for most off road riding, and especially for those routes on trails. BMX bikes could be ridden on some of the shorter rides.

For a general guide to buying all types of bicycles, consult *The Complete Book of Bicycling* by E.A. Sloane (New York: Simon and Shuster, 1988). Rob van de Plas's *The Mountain Bike Book* (San Francisco: Bicycle Books, 1988) offers good advice on purchasing that kind of bicycle, including fitting the bike.

Most larger towns in Manitoba have a sporting goods or department store offering some choice of road bikes, mountain bikes or BMX bikes. Prefer the sporting goods or specialty shop to the department store: staff are often more knowledgeable, and better repair and maintenance services are offered.

Renting Bicycles and Bike Touring

Very few businesses in Manitoba rent bicycles; consult the yellow pages, especially in Winnipeg, for current listings. A few bicycle rentals are appearing in provincial parks, such as Hecla Island and Spruce Woods. Check with Manitoba Natural Resources, Parks Branch for the status of these. Commercial bike tours are also rare. At the time of writing, only one tour operator was leading mountain bike trips in Riding Mountain National Park. Look in the Accommodation Guide published by Travel Manitoba for outfitters (see 'Getting Further Information').

Transporting Bicycles

Cycling directly from your back door is convenient, but in a province the size of Manitoba it limits the range of exploration. Consider the options for carrying bikes in and on trucks and cars. Try Tom Cuthbertson's *Bike Tripping* for graphic illustrations (Berkeley: Ten Speed Press, 1984). Transporting your bike by bus, train or plane also requires special care and a bike box.

Maintenance and Repairs

Maintaining your bike prolongs its life: simple things such as keeping tires inflated and the chain lubricated reduce pedaling resistance. Knowing how to change a flat tire, realign your chain, and make minor adjustments can also improve your cycling enjoyment. On even a short bop to Birds Hill or a spin around the cottage roads at Lester Beach, carry a spare inner tube, tire irons, a pump, and a few Allen keys which fit your seat post and handlebars. As you begin touring, or venturing on long or remote mountain bike explorations, your repertoire of repairs and tools should also increase (or cycle with someone more experienced than you!).

If mechanical aspects are not your forte, take your bike into specialty shops for repairs or maintenance. Talk to the shop owner on a slow day, when he or she has time to show you a few basic tips. Shops or cycling organizations sometimes offer courses on repairs, as may community recreation departments. Check with the Manitoba Cycling Association (see 'Getting Involved') for suggestions. Numerous books offer advice and illustrations. Very different styles are demonstrated in Bicycling Magazine's *Complete Guide to Bicycle Maintenance and Repair* (Emmaus: Rodale Press, 1986), and *Anybody's Bike Book: An Original Manual of Bicycle Repairs* by T. Cuthbertson (Berkeley: Ten Speed Press, 1984). Several condensed manuals are available to carry with you.

Basic Riding Skills

Getting on a bike and pedaling is enough to go and enjoy Manitoba, but your enjoyment and your safety can be enhanced by building cycling skills. On roads, that refers to following traffic rules and cycling defensively. Brush up with *Effective Cycling* by J. Forrester (Cambridge: MIT-Press, 1984), or contact the Manitoba Cycling Association for details about skills clinics. The Association also has information on safe cycling programs for children. Build off road riding skills by cycling with more experienced riders, and by experimenting. Several recent books and magazines discuss off road skills.

Regardless of where you are going, always cycle prepared. Carry water, snacks (or money to buy snacks), maps and tools. Inevitably the time you forget them is the time you need them. Consider wearing a helmet for both road and off road riding. For off road riding, remember your wilderness etiquette: carry your garbage out and respect other trail users.

Riding for Fitness and Racing

The virtues of cycling as exercise and recreation have been frequently extolled, and are true. Interest in racing in Manitoba has been spurred by the success of Canadian and American racers in premiere events such as the Tour de France and the Olympics. Armchair cycle with Bicycling Magazine's *Fitness through Cycling* and *Ride Like a Pro* (Emmaus: Rodale Press, 1988), then get out there and pedal. Racing and fitness oriented cycling organizations are discussed under 'Getting Started.'

Mountain Biking and Cycletouring

Suggestions for these aspects of cycling are provided in the introductions to the Paved Road and Off Road sections. Cycletouring in particular requires planning and preparation. See 'Getting Started' for clubs and organizations of fellow mountain bikers and cycletourers. A good book on mountain biking is Rob Van der Plas's *The Mountain Bike Book* (San Francisco: Bicycle Books, 1988). Van der Plas also wrote an excellent touring guide, *The Bicycle Touring Manual* (San Francisco: Bicycle Books, 1987), but there are numerous other books available. For touring food, experiment with *Feeding Your Inner Tube* by Laureen Hefferon (Berkeley: Ten Speed Press, 1983). Happy trails.

Getting Involved

Enjoy cycling in Manitoba as a solitary pursuit, in the company of friends and family, or through the activities of clubs and organizations across the province. Get involved in all aspects of riding, including recreational day rides, long distance touring, mountain biking and racing. Involvement encompasses activities out of the saddle, including social events, race officiating, safety advocacy and education.

The Manitoba Cycling Association (MCA) is an umbrella organization for cycling in the province, with a mandate to develop and promote all aspects of the sport. The MCA assists clubs through coordination and promotion of events, and provides clubs and individuals with insurance and with a connection to the national organization, the Canadian Cycling Association (CCA). Educational programs for schools, and clinics on safe riding skills, officiating and coaching are among the activities transmitted from the CCA to the MCA. The MCA prepares a handbook annually, providing current information on clubs and events.

Each of the several cycling clubs in Winnipeg specializes in a different aspect of the sport. The Winnipeg Bicycling Club Inc. (WBC) is the oldest club, and focuses on racing. Join the club for track, road and time trial competition. Well known activities of the WBC include Wednesday evening time trails at Birds Hill Provincial Park, Thursday evening track league, the Coors Cobblestone Classic, and the Canada Day Criterium at Assiniboine Park. There are several other racing clubs or teams in Winnipeg, sponsored by businesses, but membership is by invitation.

The Winnipeg Cycletouring Club (WCC) organizes recreational evening rides, day rides, and tours for beginning and experienced cycletourers. Tours explore Manitoba on two or three day trips averaging 50 to 100 km per day. Tours may be supported by a van, or cyclists may be required to carry panniers and all their equipment.

Ride and Glide is a relatively new Winnipeg club, providing recreational group riding and fitness programs. Some activities are oriented to Masters cyclists (25 years and older). The emphasis is not on competition, but regular time trials and road races are held.

The Cyclopathic Party of Winnipeg advocates designated bicycle routes for Winnipeg and better bicycle parking in the downtown area. Safety, through obeying vehicle laws, is also a key concern of the cyclopaths.

The growth of mountain biking has resulted in the Winnipeg Mountain Biking Club. Although very embryonic at the time of writing, the club may offer both recreational and racing mountain biking.

Several cycling clubs service communities outside of Winnipeg, principally in Brandon and Thompson. The Brandon Bicycling Club (BBC) offers time trials, road races and mountain biking events. The annual Brandon Hills Mountain Bike Race has been growing steadily. The Thompson Cycling Club

(TCC) promotes all forms of cycling in northern Manitoba. Members participate in club rides, tours, races, mountain biking, clinics and workshops. A new club is rumored to be underway in Flin Flon. Also in northern Manitoba, the Kelsey Recreation Centre in The Pas organizes the Northern Cycle Tour (p.46).

Several other organizations in Manitoba include cycling in their activities. The Manitoba Naturalist Society sponsors guided mountain bike rides among its many outdoor activities. The Westman Wilderness Society of Brandon is a group of enthusiastic mountain bikers who particularly enjoy Riding Mountain National Park. The Canadian Hostelling Association, Manitoba Inc., based in Winnipeg, includes day rides, tours, and clinics among its activities.

Contact the MCA for current information on clubs across the province, and to obtain contact names and phone numbers. Talk to the MCA about activities of general interest to all cyclists, and non-cycling participation at events. The MCA is a member of the Manitoba Sports Federation, and can be reached at 1700 Ellice Ave., Winnipeg, Manitoba, R3H 0B1.

Getting Further Information

Maps

Detailed mapping is provided for each route in this book. Several types of supplemental maps are mentioned in route descriptions where appropriate. A provincial highway map is essential for paved and gravel road riding, and for general orientation within the province (available free from Travel Manitoba; addresses below). Municipal road maps give details on provincial and municipal roads, and are useful for gravel road exploring. Some of the maps are 10 or more years out of date (available for a fee from the Drafting Section, Manitoba Department of Highways). Cyclists in Winnipeg will find the Cyclist's Map of Winnipeg helpful in selecting bike paths and roads with less traffic (available free from Travel Manitoba or the Manitoba Cycling Association).

Topographic maps show roads and some trails, plus contours and geographic details. Occasionally topographic maps are recommended for off road or gravel road riding, and map numbers are provided in the text. Topographic maps are available in two scales: 1:50,000 (more detailed), and 1:250,000. If using them to devise new routes not covered here, check the publication dates carefully: updating is in progress, but some are very old and inaccurate (available for a fee from Manitoba Natural Resources, Surveys and Mapping, or any outlet of topographic maps in Canada). Air photos are available for a fee from the same source in Manitoba, and are usually more current for off road route planning.

Manitoba Natural Resources also prepares Game Hunting Area Maps, showing Designated Vehicle Routes for hunters. These are updated annually, so the road and trail information for provincial parks and backwoods areas are usually detailed and current. Note that not all areas of Manitoba are mapped and that some routes involve crossing lakes or wetlands (available free from the Communications Branch, Manitoba Natural Resources).

Tourist Information

Travel Manitoba is the provincial government department responsible for tourist information. Several colorful booklets are prepared on the province, including one on parks and outdoor adventures. An overview of the province is provided in the annual Manitoba Vacation Planner. The most detailed information is available in the Accommodation Guide, which includes campgrounds, hotels, Bed and Breakfast (B&B), farm vacations and outfitters (note that many farm vacations operate as overnight B&B). Obtain these publications and others from Travel Manitoba.

The province is divided into eight tourism regions, each represented by a branch of the Tourism Industry Association. Each region prepares an information booklet with more details on attractions and facilities within each region. Obtain these through Travel Manitoba.

Background on the Province

Cyclists looking for historical and cultural information on Manitoba will find several overview histories, plus many books on the history of specific localities within the province. Check local bookstores, many of which have a Manitoba or Western Canada section, or try the Legislative Library or the public libraries. For history, browse through *Manitoba, the Province and the People* by K. Coates and F. McGuiness (Edmonton: Hurtig Publishers, 1987). *Section Lines: A Manitoba Anthology* (M. Duncan, ed.; Winnipeg: Turnstone Press, 1988) is a recent introduction to the literature of the province.

The best background information for cyclists interested in expanding their natural history and ecological understanding is found in *Natural Heritage of Manitoba: Legacy of the Ice Age* (J.T. Teller, ed.; Winnipeg: Manitoba Museum of Man and Nature, 1984). A variety of geographical, biological, economic and social information is mapped in the *Atlas of Manitoba* (T. Weir, ed.; Winnipeg: Manitoba Department of Natural Resources, 1983). For plant, bird and animal identification, refer to prairie or North American guidebooks.

Other Manitoba Cycling Descriptions

Very little information is available on other routes or areas for cycling. Alex Narvey published *Winnipeg by Cycle* (Winnipeg: Thunder Enlightening Press, 1987), with routes for that city. Three books on cycling in Canada mention Manitoba, but with little detail: Elliott Katz, *The Complete Guide to Bicycling In Canada* (Toronto: Doubleday Canada, 1987); Bruce Leaden, *Bicycle Camping in Canada* (Winnipeg: Queenston House Publishing Co., 1984); and *The Great Canadian Bicycle Trail* by G. White, A. Vine and P. Gruer (Runge Press Ltd., 1976).

Addresses

Travel Manitoba
Room 101, Legislative Building
450 Broadway Ave.
Winnipeg, Manitoba R3C 0V8

Manitoba Natural Resources
Surveys and Mapping Branch
1007 Century St.
Winnipeg, Manitoba R3H 0W4

Drafting Section
Manitoba Department of Highways
14th Floor-215 Gary St.
Winnipeg, Manitoba R3C 3Z1

Communications Branch
Manitoba Natural Resources
Box 22, 1495 St. James Ave.
Winnipeg, Manitoba R3H 0W9

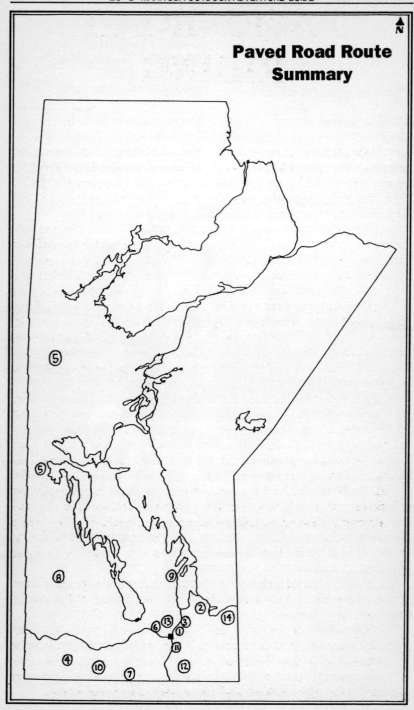

Paved Road Route Summary

PAVED ROAD RIDING

Explore the pleasures of paved road pedaling in Manitoba. Ride the smooth surface beside northern lakes, through jack pine and aspen, down the hills of the escarpment, and across fields of yellow canola to the beaches of the big lakes. Find pockets of prairie, cruise the remnants of ghost towns, and ease out of the saddle to enjoy the comforts of Manitoba's towns and cities.

Fourteen paved road routes are described in this section, followed by a summary of extended touring across Manitoba. Selected on the basis of their scenery and topography, the routes cover most regions of the province. Cycle the paved roads for recreation and family outings, or for training and fitness. Select day rides, short tours, or extended trips of two weeks or more around the province. Chalk up a century ride (100 miles in one day) along PTH 26.

Under each of the 14 route headings, several recommended rides may be described. Some are day rides; many are tours with delightful day rides along portions of the routes. Skim through the descriptions, or refer to the overview map and the summary table (p.22) to select a ride which suits your cycling ability, as well as your riding and geographical interests.

The route descriptions are structured similarly to the Gravel Road and Off Road sections (see p.7, 'How to Use this Book'). Where there are several options under one major heading, tours are usually listed first. Suggestions for day rides and ways to extend the tours are listed at the end of most major routes. For tours, the possibilities for either cycle camping or traveling 'fast-and-light' (carrying less equipment and staying in hotels or B&B) are discussed. Facilities are also listed for each town en route, in addition to the overview provided under the 'Facilities' paragraph. 'Full facilities' indicates that a center has stores, restaurants, camping and hotels. For the tours, a distance is included beside the facilities listing of each town: these are the kilometers from the last town, unless otherwise noted. Traffic levels are also described.

The majority of paved highways in Manitoba have gravel shoulders. Information on current road conditions can be obtained through the provincial department of highways.

Wind is an important element of road cycling in Manitoba (p.10). It can turn a pleasant jaunt into an endurance test. If you have the flexibility, listen to forecasts, and adjust your route accordingly. Riding in a group and drafting each other provides some relief. And if the wind really gets you down, vary your road riding with a little off road adventuring in sheltered forests.

Paved Road Routes Summaries

A. Listed Alphabetically (as they appear in the book)

(The numbers peceding the route names represent their locations on the Summary Map.)

1. Birds Hill Bop / 25
2. Forest and Falls / 29
3. Lockport Loop / 33
4. Mouse and Turtle Tour / 36
5. Northern Parks Tour / 41
6. PTH 26 and Headingley / 49
7. PTH 31 to Windygates / 51
8. Riding Mountain Circle / 54
9. The Road to Hecla / 58

10. Rock Lake Tour / 62
11. St. Adolphe and
    St. Norbert / 65
12. St. Malo Tour / 68
13. Stonewall Starter Tour / 70
14. The Whiteshell / 73

15. Extended Touring across
    Manitoba / 78

B. Listed Geographically

Winnipeg and Selkirk:
Birds Hill Bop
Lockport Loop
PTH 26 and Headingley
St. Adolphe and St. Norbert
Stonewall Starter Tour

Eastern:
Forest and Falls
St. Malo Tour
The Whiteshell

Central and Southwestern:
Mouse and Turtle Tour
PTH 31 to Windygates
Rock Lake Tour

Interlake:
The Road to Hecla

Parklands:
Riding Mountain Circle
Northern Parks Tour

North:
Northern Parks Tour

C. Listed by Difficulty

(The symbol + denotes that the ride is also found in a harder category)

Easy:
Birds Hill Bop (from Selkirk) +
Birds Hill Bop (in and around park)
Forest and Falls (family tour)
Lockport Loop
PTH 26 and Headingley +
St. Adolphe +
Stonewall Starter
The Road to Hecla +
Whiteshell (circle tour) +

Moderate:
Birds Hill Bop (from Winnipeg)
Birds Hill Bop (from Selkirk)
Forest and Falls (via Stead)
Mouse and Turtle Tour
    (from Brandon)
Northern Parks Tour (north) +
PTH 26 and Headingley
PTH 31
Riding Mountain (short)
Riding Mountain (long) +
Rock Lake Tour
St Adolphe
St. Malo Tour
The Road to Hecla
Whiteshell (circle)
Whiteshell (from Winnipeg) +
Cross Manitoba +

Difficult:
Mouse and Turtle Tour (from
    Glenboro)
Northern Parks Tour (south)
Northern Parks Tour (north)
Riding Mountain (long)
Whiteshell (from Winnipeg)
Cross Manitoba

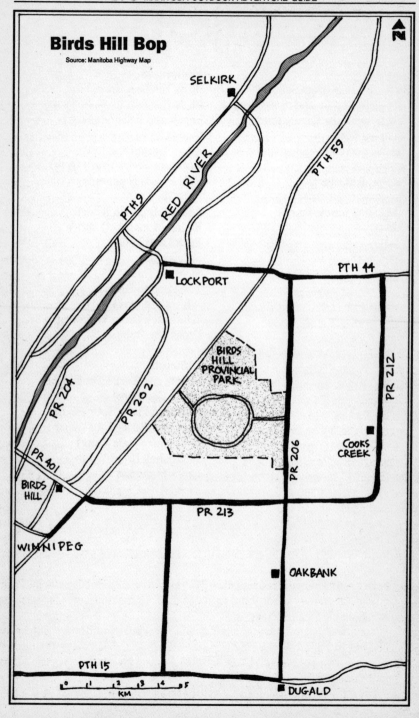

Birds Hill Bop

Source: Manitoba Highway Map

The Birds Hill Bop

Birds Hill Provincial Park has long served a variety of recreational needs. For cyclists, it offers a quick escape into the country from either Winnipeg or Selkirk. Ride a circle route to the park in a day, or cycle a shorter distance out-and-back. Find further distance and variety by combining the Bop with the Lockport Loop (p.33) or the River Road Heritage Parkway (p.95). Alternatively, avoid the heavy city traffic by transporting bikes to Birds Hill, where the cruising is good in and around the park. Overnight camping at the park turns the Birds Hill Bop into a tour; it is also part of the Stonewall Starter Tour (p.70).

The choice of routes includes flat, straight city roads, winding riverside drives, and a hilly, forested section of road which salves the flat-prairie-blues. This is one of the classic rides in the Winnipeg-Selkirk area, and serves equally well as a good training run for serious cyclists, or a day of fun for families. Combine the ride with the other recreational facilities of Birds Hill Provincial Park, or events such as the annual Winnipeg Folk Festival.

Riding from Winnipeg

Type: Paved road day rides or tours.
Access: Begins and ends in Winnipeg. From Winnipeg, consult the Cyclist's Map of Winnipeg to find best connection to the start of the three possible routes: Raleigh Road, Dugald Road, and Henderson Highway.
Facilities: Stores and restaurants within Winnipeg. Picnic sites, campgrounds and snack bar in Birds Hill Provincial Park.
Distance: One-way distances to East Gate of Birds Hill Provincial Park from Winnipeg's Perimeter Highway by various routes as follows:

via Raleigh St.	12 km
via Henderson Highway	14 km
via PTH 115	19 km

Difficulty: Easy to moderate (easy to moderate distance; easy hills).

There are three main routes from Winnipeg to Birds Hill Provincial Park. Cyclists can choose to ride there and back on the same route, or ride one route out and a different one home.

One route out of town is via Raleigh St. heading northeast from East Kildonan to Highway 101 (the Perimeter Highway). Nip along the narrow track at the end of Raleigh St. to cross Highway 101, and join Sperring Ave. which runs parallel to the main highway. Swing north (left) on this road as it follows PTH 59 and becomes Birds Hill Road. Turn east (right) at Camsell

Ave., then dip down to join PTH 59. Follow this heavily traveled highway for 2.6 km to the junction with PR 213 (east/right turn).

PR 213 marks the transition to a rural ride. Just east of the junction with PR 207, short hills rise, the product of a glacial esker. Whirl up and down past the gravel pits; during weekdays be alert for gravel trucks. At the junction with PR 206 swing north (left), and roll with the hills to the east gate of Birds Hill Provincial Park.

The second route follows Henderson Highway past the Perimeter Highway. Turn east (right) at the Pritchard Farm Road or further north at PR 401, and follow either road across the tracks to Birds Hill Road. Turn north (left) from Pritchard Farm Road or south (right) from PR 401, and cycle to Camsell Ave. Then follow the above route.

The final choice is to cycle on Dugald Road straight eastward, as it becomes PR 115. Turn north (left) on PR 207, just over the floodway, and travel to the junction with PR 213. Turn east (right) onto PR 213, and continue as described above. A slight variation is to continue further west on PR 115 to PR 206 at Dugald, turn north (left), then ride straight up 206 to the East Gate. Traffic is heavy on PR 115.

Riding from Selkirk

Type: Paved road day rides or tours.
Access: Begins and ends in downtown Selkirk on Main St. where PR 204 leads off to the east.
Facilities:: Stores and restaurants in Selkirk and Lockport. Picnic sites, campgrounds and snack bar in Birds Hill Provincial Park.
Distance: Direct route is 34 km one way. Alternate return is 55 km one way.
Difficulty: Moderate (moderate distance; easy hills).

From Selkirk take PR 204 across the Red River, and pedal this beautiful winding road southward, past long, narrow riverfront fields. At the cloverleaf east of Lockport (12 km), select PTH 44 east, following it over bustling PTH 59. It's a few more turns of the crank to the junction with PR 206, where you turn south (right), then glide to the East Gate.

Return to Selkirk by the same route, or make a loop by traveling south from the East Gate (right turn) on PR 206, west (right) on PR 213, briefly south (left) on PTH 59 to the first turnoff after the floodway. Follow this road to the T-junction, turn north (right) on PR 202 through the town of Birds Hill. Swing west (left) on PR 401 to PR 204 (Henderson Highway), then turn north (right). Follow this riverside road through Lockport, jogging east (right) to the cloverleaf, then north and home.

Bopping In and Around the Park

Type: Paved road day rides.
Access: Within Birds Hill Provincial Park, there are many designated parking areas. Parking at East Beach or West Beach is recommended for best access to all routes within the park. The Pine Ridge Bicycle Trail is also accessible from the campground or the riding stable.
Facilities: Picnic sites, campgrounds and snack bar at riding stable and in campground. Water and washrooms along Pine Ridge Bicycle Trail.
Distance: Several routes are suggested as follows:

North and South Drives	11 km
Group Use Road	5 km
Pine Ridge Bicycle Path	7 km
Cooks Creek Loop	19 km

Difficulty: Easy (distances and hills).

The circular park road is divided into the North Drive and the South Drive. Together they describe a gracious loop past aspen and oak forests, and by flower-sprinkled meadows fringed by spruce. The biggest hills are along the eastern segment, between the campground and the riding stables. This route is used by the Winnipeg Bicycle Club in weekly Wednesday evening races.

The Pine Ridge Bicycle Trail curves and twists for 7 hilly km as it circles the man-made lake. Coast past the beaches, work up the twisting climbs through tall aspen forests, and breathe deeply through three magnificent stretches of scented pines. A branch of the trail heads north across the main park road, ending in a T-junction. To the east (right) are the stables, to the west (left) is a connection to the Group Use Road.

The 5 km Group Use Road is a good choice for cyclists. Traffic is one-way around the loop, which is often closed to cars in the spring and fall. Cruise the few gradual and gentle hills, passing open prairie, rows of chokecherries and the characteristic oak and aspen forests.

Chalk up more km along a pleasant circular route from the East Gate of the park. For cycling counterclockwise, the sequence of directions from the gate is: south (right) on PR 206; east (left) on PR 213; north (left) on PR 212; west (left) on PTH 44; south (left) on PR 206 back to the gate. The highlight of this ride is the Grotto of Our Lady of Lourdes and the adjacent Ukrainian Catholic church at Cooks Creek on PR 212 (12 km; store). PR 206 is the hilliest road, with thick oaks clothing the view to the west. The rest of the ride is pleasantly rural, with lots of trees to break up the horizon.

And finally, discover the many hours of mountain biking pleasure along the ski trails and snowmobile routes of Birds Hill Provincial Park (see p.123).

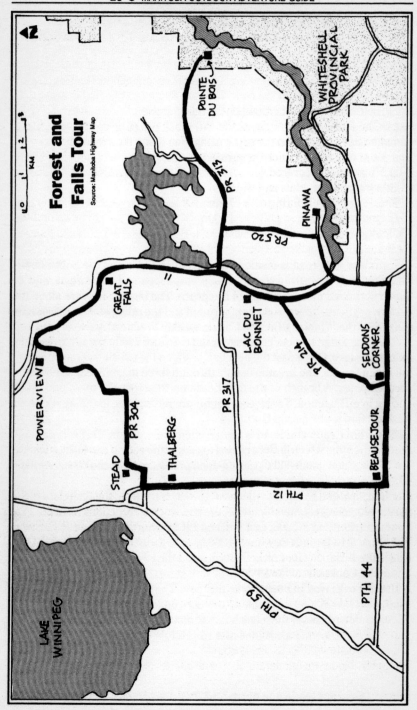

Forest and Falls Tour

Source: Manitoba Highway Map

Forest and Falls Tour

Northeast of Beausejour, in eastern Manitoba, stretches a region of varied forests bounded by the falls of the Winnipeg River. Near the river, the Canadian Shield thrusts to the surface. Further south, the Precambrian rocks have been coated with thick deposits from the glaciers, sculpting high sand ridges, now thickly covered with jack pines. Closer to Beausejour, croplands mingle with aspens, elms and willows.

This is wonderful touring country. Forests and falls supply superb scenery; rocks and sand ridges add hills and turns. A network of good roads with little traffic provides a selection of circular routes of varied distance and difficulty. Facilities are adequate, with a choice of camping or fast-and-light touring.

Two touring routes are described below, plus connections with other routes for a longer cycling holiday. The first route cuts north from Beausejour to Stead, then follows the Winnipeg River before returning to Beausejour. This is a trip with long daily distances for experienced riders. The second route is a shorter two-day tour west from Beausejour, with lots of time for rest and relaxation along the Winnipeg River. This tour is recommended for families and beginning cycletourers.

Winnipeg River via Stead

Type: Paved road tours.
Access: Tour based from Beausejour in eastern Manitoba. Leave via PTH 12 north from the eastern end of town; the tour returns to the east end via PTH 44.
Facilities: Moderate distance between towns, some with complete facilities, all with stores or restaurants. Most frequent facilities along the Winnipeg River.
Distance: Two or three day tours are suggested as follows:
Alternative I: two day tour of 180 km:

day 1- Beausejour to Powerview	90 km
day 2- Powerview to Beausejour	90 km

Alternative II: Extended three day tour of 252 km:

day 1- Beausejour to Powerview	90 km
day 2- Powerview to Pointe du Bois	78 km
day 3- Pointe du Bois to Beausejour	84 km

Difficulty: Moderate (moderate distances and hills).

From Beausejour, cycle due north on PTH 12 for 50 km. Although straight, with only gentle undulations, the pedaling is pleasurable across the rural landscape of fields and trees. Stop at the 'tea room' museum in Ladywood for a break from the bike. At the junction with PR 304 turn east (right; store and picnic facilities) to the hills and turns of PR 304.

From Stead (48 km; full facilities except camping), continue east and north along PR 304 all the way to the junction with PTH 11 (31 km). Initially the road crosses a straight plain of sod farms, bounded on two sides by low sand ridges: Belair Provincial Forest behind, and Brightstone Sandhills ahead. Once the latter is reached, the pleasures of this tour really kick in. Now the road bends, turns, and pops over gentle rises. There is a wilderness feel here, with Precambrian granite breaking through, and the anticipation of a deer or coyote appearing around a corner. Near the junction with PTH 11 are the towns of Powerview and Pine Falls (full facilities, including camping and accommodation at Maskwa Lodge), and the first contact with the Winnipeg River.

The Pine Falls Generating Station is the most downstream of six hydroelectric dams capturing the Winnipeg River's energy. Leaving Pine Falls, pedal southeast on PTH 11. The first 30 km along this highway are among the loveliest of the tour, with frequent river vistas among the cottages, towns and pastures. St. George (7 km from Pine Falls; stores, restaurant) has a holiday town feel, with a tempting swimming beach. Just outside Great Falls (15 km; stores, restaurants), a wayside park sits near the Great Falls Generating Station. A second wayside park waits south of McArthur Generating Station, and a third overlooks the southwestern shore of Lac du Bonnet. From here, the main road leaves the river, but the many transmission lines maintain the connection. A back road entrance to the town of Lac du Bonnet turns east (left) at PR 313 for about one km, then south (right) onto PR 502. The road skirts the river into town (20 km; full facilities, including lodges).

To return to Beausejour from Lac du Bonnet, cycle south on PR 502. At the junction with PTH 11, turn south (left) onto the main highway. It is a short ride, with a last glimpse of the river, to the junction with PR 214 (5 km). Turn southwest (right) onto this road, stopping to replenish your water bottles at the signposted spring water, 3 km along the road. The next 27 km along PR 214 cross Agassiz Provincial Forest, climbing up the sandy spine of the ancient glacial beach ridge. The descent to Seddons Corner is a joy, with a panorama to the west, and a jumble of jack pines to the east.

Seddons Corner marks the junction with PTH 44 (store and restaurant). Take a last glance at the hills of Agassiz behind you, and turn west (right) onto the flat, straight ride back to agricultural Manitoba and Beausejour (16 km). Most of the way, the old highway parallels the new, trading very little traffic for the occasional gravel patch or detour.

Tack additional kilometers onto this tour by veering east (left) onto PR 313, just before the town of Lac du Bonnet. Follow the curves and the transmission lines as far as you want through this cottage country. There are several campsites and lodges on the way to the end of the road at Pointe du Bois (36 km from PR 502; full facilities), where the most upstream of the generating stations operates. Relax in this Canadian Shield playground before backtracking to PTH 11. An alternate route back to Beausejour would be to follow the return route of the short tour (see below).

Family and Relaxation Tour

Type: Paved road tours (an alternate return requires approximately 17 km of gravel road riding).
Access: Tour begins and ends on PTH 44, east from Beausejour.
Facilities: Seddons Corner only facilities (store and restaurant) between Beausejour and Lac du Bonnet. More frequent but scattered facilities along PR 313.
Distance: A two day tour between 106 and 125 km as follows:
    day 1- Beausejour to Lac du Bonnet   48 km
    day 2- Lac du Bonnet to Beausejour   58 or 77 km
Cycling along PR 313 can add up to 72 km (return).
Difficulty: Easy to moderate (easy distances; moderate hills).

From Beausejour, cycle east along PTH 44, keeping to the old highway to avoid traffic. At Seddons Corner (16 km; store and restaurant) fuel up, then turn north (left) onto PR 214 in Agassiz Provincial Forest. Climb the former glacial shores, then freewheel down to the junction with PTH 11. Turn north (left) and continue along the river to the junction with PR 502, veering right, and traveling northeast to the town of Lac du Bonnet (48 km; full facilities including lodges). Cycling additional distance along PR 313 opens up further opportunities for camping and lodges along the Lee River.

There are two choices for returning on the second day. If you are riding a mountain bike or a touring bike which can handle gravel roads, ride along PR 313 to the junction with the recently completed PR 520. Turn south. Halfway along the road is the fascinating Pinawa Dam Provincial Heritage Park. Explore the stoic and silent ruins of the first dam constructed on the Winnipeg River system. Further south at PR 211 turn west (right) back to PTH 11. Alternately, leave Lac du Bonnet on PTH 11, or return along PR 313 to PTH 11 and travel south (left turn).

From the junction of PTHs 211 and 11, pedal south for 5 km. The tall silhouette of the powerhouse and spillway gates at Seven Sisters Hydroelectric Generating Station announces the junction with PR 307. It's worth the short side trip to the picnic site by the dam, and the walk across the top of the sluiceway.

Continue south on PTH 11 to the junction with PTH 44 (5 km). Swing west (right) at the junction, returning to the jack pines of Agassiz Provincial Forest. A picnic spot (7 km) has toilets and water. Enjoy the descent down to Seddons Corner, then the final 16 km spin into Beausejour.

Day Rides and Tour Extensions

The roads of the tour routes are suitable for day rides. Three segments are particularly recommended: PTH 11 between Pine Falls and Lac du Bonnet; all of PR 313; and PR 214 through Agassiz Provincial Forest.

There are two ready ways to extend these short tours into four to seven day outings. Camping or fast-and-light travel are possible in all cases. Leaving from and returning to Winnipeg immediately tacks on two days. Winnipeg to Beausejour is approximately 65 km one way, traveling via the Lockport Loop (p.33), then straight east along PTH 44. Extend the tour further by cycling through the Whiteshell Provincial Park. Add one or two days of beautiful scenery and hilly curving roads along PR 307 (p.75).

For those with mountain bikes, spice up the paved road touring with a little off road riding. Check out the trails in Belair Provincial Forest (p.117), Agassiz Provincial Forest (p.115), and Whiteshell Provincial Park (p.187).

The Lockport Loop and Lower Fort Garry

This pleasurable day trip from Winnipeg emphasizes both the scenery and the history of the Red River. Ride it just for the exercise, or make it into a family outing with lots of stops, culminating in a picnic at Lower Fort Garry. Combine the Lockport Loop with the Birds Hill Bop (p.25) or the River Road Heritage Ride (p.95) for further variety and distance.

Type: Paved road day rides.
Access: Begin and end in Winnipeg. Consult the Cyclist's Map of Winnipeg for best route to/from both Henderson Highway and Main Street at the Perimeter Highway. Designated parking lot for Henderson Highway bicycle route immediately north of Perimeter Highway.
Facilities: Restaurants and stores in Lockport. Restaurant, washrooms and water at Lower Fort Garry. Occasional restaurants and stores along rest of route.
Distance: 42 km return of level riding, including 12 km loop return to Lower Fort Garry.
Difficulty: Easy (distances and hills).

After the Perimeter Highway of Winnipeg, the Henderson Highway becomes PR 204. This is a designated bicycle route, with a wide paved shoulder which curves northward with the river. Grab glimpses of the river and the historic buildings on the opposite bank.

Lockport (18 km) is announced by several well-known ice-cream and snack outlets. Continue refreshed to the junction with PTH 44, and turn west (left) to cross the St. Andrews Locks on the Red River, operated to maintain navigable water levels in Winnipeg.

Just off the locks, turn north (right) on River Road for a pleasant pedal beside stately columns of elms and a view of the broad, concrete mouth of the Red River Floodway. The road curves to join PTH 9, then it is only a few km north (right turn) to Lower Fort Garry. This national historic park particularly merits a visit from June to August and during the weekends of September, when Parks Canada staff replicate the fur trading days of the late 1880s.

To complete the loop to Winnipeg, travel straight south on PTH 9 (20 km from Lower Fort Garry), although traffic is heavy on this road. An alternative is to ride part of the way along the River Road Heritage Parkway (p.95), or to retrace your route back along Henderson Highway.

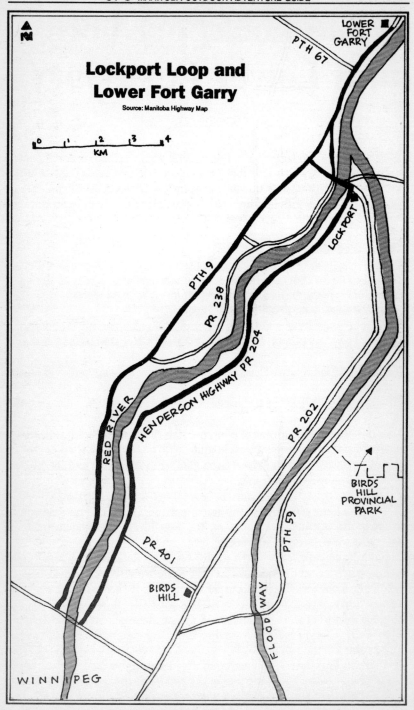

Lockport Loop and Lower Fort Garry

Source: Manitoba Highway Map

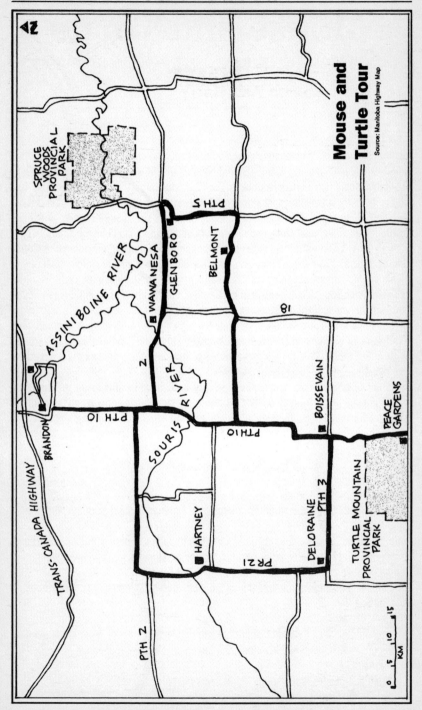

Mouse and
Turtle Tour

Source: Manitoba Highway Map

Mouse and Turtle Tour

In southwestern Manitoba, the Souris ('mouse' in French) River cuts a meandering 'S' through the glacial moraine and underlying shales, while further south the more resistant Turtle Mountains rise. Between the two stretch many kilometers of good cycletouring through some of Manitoba's best rural scenery. Long hills test endurance at the northern and southern ends of the tour, and the steep walls of the Souris River valley pose further challenges. The rest of the ride rolls across an undulating landscape with few flat sections. Pass dense woodlands, pastures and grain fields. There are clusters of communities and exhilarating open stretches with only an occasional farmhouse. This beautiful and varied tour invites and challenges at any time of the cycletouring season.

Most of the tour follows seldom-traveled roads, all in good condition. Cyclists can either camp or travel fast-and-light, with B&B or hotel accommodation available. This tour is best suited to intermediate and expert cycletourers because of the long daily distances.

Choose one of two tours. A three day spin begins and ends in Brandon, while a tour with longer daily distances is based in Glenboro. Possibilities abound for day rides, tour extensions, and off road riding along the route.

The Brandon Based Tour

Type: Paved road tours.
Access: Tour begins and ends in Brandon. Follow PTH 10 south out of the city.
Facilities: Infrequent towns, most with full facilities. Carry sufficient food and water for each day. Reservations for indoor accommodation especially recommended in fall, because of the influx of hunters.
Distance: Total distance of 231 or 261 km over hilly terrain as follows:
Alternative I
    day 1- Brandon to Hartney   82 km
    day 2- Hartney to Adam Lake   84 km
    day 3- Adam Lake to Brandon   95 km
Alternative II
    day 1- Brandon to Hartney   82 km
    day 2- Hartney to Boissevain   75 km

day 3- Boissevain to Brandon   74 km
Difficulty: Moderate (distances and hills).

South of Brandon on PTH 10, the Brandon Hills rise east to west across the highway. The road first drops to cross the Little Souris River, then, with a mixture of steep and gradual climbs, 760 m are gained over the next 12 km.

At the junction with PTH 2 (24 km; store, restaurant), turn west (right). The highway initially skirts a slough wrapped by aspens and oaks, then climbs to a plateau that very gently rolls past grain and oilseed fields to Souris. The town of Souris (22 km; full facilities) merits a visit. Perched along the steep walls of its namesake river, Souris boasts the longest swinging bridge in Canada, a museum in a mansion, and a 'rock hound' pit. Victoria Park is a wonderful place to relax, have a picnic, or splash in the pool.

Follow PTH 2 west from Souris. This section rates as the flattest of the route, but the view is pleasantly rural, with riverbank elms along Plum Creek prominent to the north. Follow the curve of the road to the south and the next crossing of the Souris River. The Souris has lost its steep banks here, and the descent to the crossing is barely discernible. Hartney is a small, quiet town graced with tall elms (34 km; full facilities including B&B).

From Hartney, continue straight south on PTH 21 and follow it to Deloraine (36 km; full facilities), located at the junction with PTH 3. The Souris River is left behind, and part way along PTH 21 the Turtle Mountains pop up on the horizon, a blue beacon for the rest of the day's ride. The route gradually climbs as it progresses southward. There are virtually no towns with services along this section, so leave Hartney with full water bottles and lunch bags.

The ride eastward from Deloraine along PTH 3 (left turn from PTH 21) is delightful. The Turtle Mountains form a dramatic backdrop to the south, and there are wonderful panoramas to the north: in the summer, a brilliant checkerboard of yellow canola, blue flax and green hills. Whitewater Lake shimmers to the north, attracting thousands of migrating geese.

After 34 km of pedaling, the junction with PTH 10 is reached. If you need supplies, the closest source is Boissevain, 6 km to the north (left; full facilities including B&B). Campers should cycle south (right) on PTH 10 to the Adam Lake Campground in Turtle Mountain Provincial Park. As the road climbs the 170 m into the Turtle Mountains, cropland is replaced by pastures, which fold away into forest. The Adam Lake campground (15 km) invites relaxation with a beach and superb mountain biking and hiking trails (p.185). Pedal a few more kilometers to the International Peace Garden, where several narrow but hilly roads wind around both sides of the border. The ride to Adam Lake and the Peace Garden is also a worthwhile spin for those staying in Boissevain, especially as the ride back is mostly downhill (54 km return).

The directions from Adam Lake back to Brandon are easy: cycle north on PTH 10. The only facilities are in Boissevain or at the turnoff to Souris (77 km). Despite the straight road, the scenery is varied and the landscape undulating. Several creeks are crossed, and approximately half way an old friend, the

Souris River, provides a plunging descent and a demanding ascent. After more fields, forests and uphill grunting, coast out of the Brandon Hills and into the city.

The Glenboro-based Tour

Type: Paved road tours.
Access: The tour begins and ends in Glenboro, on PTH 2, in central Manitoba.
Facilities: Infrequent towns, most with full facilities. Carry a day's supply of food and water. Reservations recommended during fall hunting season.
Distance: A tour of 317 km as follows:
  day 1- Glenboro to Hartney   113 km
  day 2- Hartney to Adam Lake   84 km
  day 3- Adam Lake to Glenboro 120 km
Difficulty: Difficult (difficult distances; moderate hills).

This tour follows much the same route described above, but by beginning in Glenboro, 45 km are added through longer first and last days. From this town (full facilities) which sports a camel statue, follow PTH 2 westward to where it joins PTH 10. While these 50 km are generally flat, straight and wide open, there are almost always hills on the horizon to watch: the Tiger Hills to the south, and further west, the Brandon Hills. Near Wawanesa (30 km from Glenboro; full facilities) there is a momentary but spectacular panorama, before the road drops into the Souris River valley. At PTH 10, turn right and climb northward for 5 km, then take the westward (left) turn of PTH 2, connecting here with the tour from Brandon. Follow the directions above to Hartney. The second day of this tour is the same as the second day of the first tour.

The third day of the long tour initially follows the Brandon-based tour northward along PTH 10. However, turn east (right) onto PTH 23, and follow it across three small tributaries of the Souris to Ninette (71 km; full facilities). Check out the beach on Pelican Lake and an ice-cream shop with a huge topographic map of the region. Continue on PTH 23 up the wall of the Pembina Valley and across the morainic undulations of the Tiger Hills to the junction with PTH 5. Swing north (left), ultimately descending to Glenboro (49 km).

Day Rides and Tour Extensions

The hills and the scenery of this tour are amenable to day rides as well as touring. Two routes are particularly recommended. Ride south from Brandon into the hills, or day tour the Turtle Mountains from Boissevain.

Extend the tour by adding further road kilometers, or by gravel road and off road riding. The loveliest paved road extension lies north of Glenboro: the spin along PTH 5 through Spruce Woods Provincial Heritage Park. Leave time to stroll the desert environment of the Spirit Sands Trail. Connect the Mouse and Turtle Tour with the Riding Mountain Circle (p.54) by riding north from Brandon on PTH 10 to Wasagaming (100 km).

Explore the gravel roads of the Lavenham Area (p.85) or the Tiger Hills (p.81). Take your mountain bikes to Spruce Woods, and enjoy the immense selection of trails (p.175). Off road pleasures are also found in the Brandon Hills (p.127), the Lauder Sandhills Wildlife Management Area near Hartney (p.143), and throughout Turtle Mountain Provincial Park (p.181).

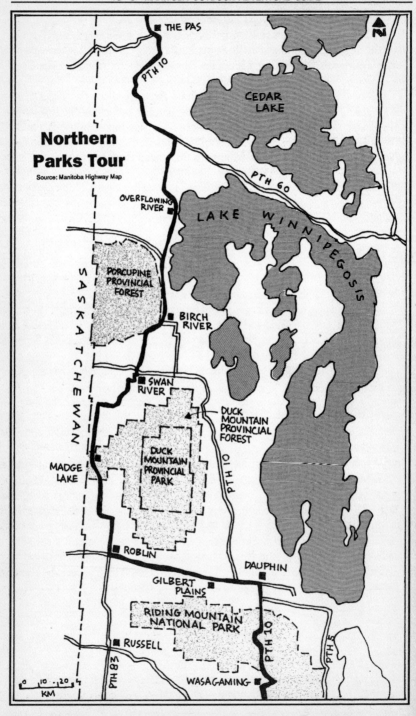

Northern Parks Tour

Source: Manitoba Highway Map

Northern Parks Tour

The Northern Parks Tour offers experienced cycletourers an unusual opportunity and challenge: long-distance touring into the wilderness of northern Manitoba. There is a range of choices from a short three day ride to an extended tour of more than 10 days, allowing cyclists to venture 'North of 53' on excellent paved highways. Pedal through kilometers of varied forests to some of the loveliest lakes in Manitoba. Traverse or parallel the distinctive 'mountains' of Manitoba in the southern kilometers of the ride. Consider cycling the most northern portion of the tour without heavy camping gear, luxuriously hopping between lakeside lodges.

As enticing as this route sounds, it is definitely for experienced cyclists only. Be prepared for long stretches without facilities or even fellow-travelers. Cyclists must be fit enough to ride to each night's destination regardless of head winds or fatigue: there often aren't any alternative lodgings or campsites. A full set of tools and the ability to use them are also a must, as is an ample supply of insect repellent. Recognizing and being prepared for all contingencies is an important part of planning for this trip, which can be one of the most rewarding rides in the province.

There are two main sections to the Northern Parks Tour: from Riding Mountain National Park to The Pas, and The Pas north. The southern half of the tour swings in a wide 'S' up and down the Manitoba Escarpment, reveling in the mixture of agricultural and wilderness scenery typical of the parkland region. Riding Mountain National Park is crossed and Duck Mountain Provincial Park skirted in the five day tour, which averages 100 km a day. Infrequent accommodations limit flexibility in this route, and camping gear is required.

From The Pas north there is greater choice in tour length, daily distances and accommodation. Four alternates are discussed below, offering a combination of camping or lodges, and short distances or long distances. Experience two more provincial parks, and a mixture of landscapes including northern deciduous forests, rocky Canadian Shield terrain, and sections of stunted spruce muskeg. Combine this northern section with the southern tour, or begin north of the 53rd parallel by driving, flying or taking the train to The Pas. Several day rides and tour extensions are also discussed.

Wasagaming to The Pas

Type: Paved road tours.
Access: The tour begins in Wasagaming, in Riding Mountain National Park, western Manitoba. The route can be ridden one way, connecting with the

northern tour at The Pas, or with return to Wasagaming by bus, or train to Dauphin then bus to Wasagaming. Alternately, return to Winnipeg via bus, train or plane. Check the most recent schedules when planning your tour.

Facilities: Limited. Infrequent towns, campgrounds and overnight accommodation. Camping required between Birch River and The Pas. Carry lots of water and extra food.

Distance: A 528 km tour, one way to The Pas, is recommended as follows:

day 1- Wasagaming to Grandview	115 km
day 2- Grandview to Madge Lake	109 km
day 3- Madge Lake to Birch River	108 km
day 4- Birch River to Overflowing River	96 km
day 5- Overflowing River to The Pas	100 km

Difficulty: Difficult (difficult distances; moderate to difficult hills).

The holiday atmosphere in Wasagaming starts the tour. Head north on PTH 10, cranking and coasting over the hills covered in spruce and aspen forests. Enjoy the paved shoulder, the 80 km/hr speed limit and the opportunity to see the park's wildlife, including deer, elk, moose, coyotes and wolves. There are frequent opportunities to stop and hike or picnic, and several interpretive trails introduce you to the local ecology. Zip down the edge of the Manitoba Escarpment and into the plain around Dauphin (70 km; full facilities). The town can be bypassed if desired by following PTH 10 as it swings west (to the left). Ignore the turn to the north, and follow PTH 5 straight west across the farmland to Gilbert Plains (30 km) and Grandview (15 km from Gilbert Plains; both full facilities). From Grandview west, you gradually gain elevation as you roll along hummocky hills and dip across rivers and streams.

At Roblin (48 km; full facilities) turn north (right) onto PTH 83, and cruise the long, gradual hills along the top of the Manitoba Escarpment. Near Madge Lake (61 km; camping), hummocky hills pop up before PTH 83 drops into the Swan River valley. After Benito (35 km; full facilities) swing east then north with the highway to Swan River (36 km; full facilities), midway between the silhouettes of Duck Mountain to the south and Porcupine Mountain to the north.

Follow PTH 10 north from Swan River (a less traveled route is PR 268). The fertile farmland of the valley stretches on either side towards Bowsman (16 km; full facilities). Swing east with the road as it skirts the wall of the escarpment. Birch River (21 km; full facilities) is the first of several logging towns marking the transition from agricultural Manitoba to a northern environment. The wayside park just before the turnoff to Birch River is a particularly delightful spot for camping.

Traveling north from Birch River, good views of the steeply rising escarpment alternate with dense forests enclosing the roadside. Stock up in Mafeking (34 km; full facilities, except camping), as the next facilities are 62 km away in Overflowing River. Continuing north on PTH 10, the hills fold away, and the last leg to The Pas is underway. The route enters a vast swamp of stunted spruce which continues past Overflowing River, a small town and campsite (no hotel) on the north end of Lake Winnipegosis. Just north of the junction with PTH 60, hop out of the swamp and onto the prominent ridge of The Pas moraine. From here to The Pas are broad sweeping curves, gentle rises and thousands and thousands of trees.

North from The Pas

Type: Paved road tours.
Access: The Pas can be reached from Winnipeg by plane, and from other areas of southern Manitoba by car, bus or train. The few roads and infrequent accommodation eliminate circle tour options. There are several possible tours, ending in Flin Flon, Snow Lake, Wekusko or Ponton. Return from Flin Flon by plane to Winnipeg, or by car or bus to The Pas. Return to The Pas or Winnipeg by train from Wekusko or Ponton. Bus service also from Snow Lake. All schedules should be confirmed during the trip planning. Plane and train reservations required. Signaling the train (mechanical button marked) is necessary to stop the train in Wekusko or Ponton.
Facilities: Infrequent towns, some more than 200 km apart. Occasional stores and lodges in between. Campers should carry at least two days supply of food. Those staying in lodges must have advance reservations for every night. All cyclists should carry several bottles of water.
Distances: There are many choices of itineraries, depending on daily distances and preferred accommodation. Several options are suggested below. Note that tours leading to Wekusko Falls could also be ended by cycling to Snow Lake, rather than Wekusko or Ponton. Alternatives A, B, and D could be extended to Thompson (see next section):

Alternative I: Long distances/Lodges or Camping
day 1- The Pas to Cranberry Portage	90 km
day 2- Cranberry to Flin Flon, and return	101 km
day 3- Cranberry to Reed Lake	80 km
day 4- Reed Lake to Ponton	102 km
or day 4- Reed Lake to Wekusko Falls	57 km
day 5- Wekusko Falls to Ponton	81 km

Alternative II: Long distances/Camping
day 1- The Pas to Simonhouse Lake	95 km
day 2- Simonhouse to Wekusko Falls	100 km
day 3- Wekusko Falls to Ponton	81 km

Alternative III: Short distances/Lodges
day 1- The Pas to Wanless	50 km
day 2- Wanless to Cranberry Portage	40 km
day 3- Cranberry Portage to Flin Flon	51 km

Alternative IV: Short distances/Camping
day 1- The Pas to Wanless	50 km

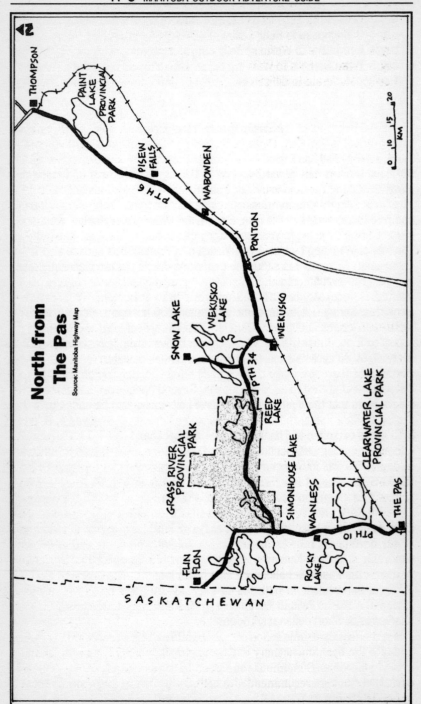

North from
The Pas

Source: Manitoba Highway Map

day 2- Wanless to Simonhouse Lake   45 km
day 3- Simonhouse to Reed Lake   43 km
day 4- Reed Lake to Wekusko Falls   57 km
day 5- Wekusko Falls to Wekusko   44 km

Difficulty: Moderate to difficult (moderate to difficult distances; moderate hills).

The initial 10 km out of The Pas are flat, but nearing Clearwater Lake Provincial Park gradual hills begin. Detour in to see the lake: its aquamarine depth is fabulous, especially on a windless day. Approximately 16 km further east on PR 287 is the short but rewarding Caves Hiking Trail. North of Clearwater Provincial Park, the landscape settles into the pattern for many of the subsequent kilometers: long, gentle hills and curves, with alternating deciduous and coniferous forests. The traffic is generally light, so cruise, and watch for deer, eagles, and great grey owls. The other denizens of this region, the mosquitoes, blackflies and deer flies, will make their appearance when you stop.

Wanless on Rocky Lake (50 km; full facilities) is the last chance in 45 km to buy supplies and fill up with well water. Picnic or camp on the shores of the pretty lake, approximately 2 km on a gravel road from the highway. Continuing from Wanless, the kilometers tick by. The many dirt roads leading off into the bush are logging roads, many actively used for clearcutting operations.

A picnic site is perched on the shores of shallow Goose Lake, one km off the highway on a gravel road (26 km; latrines, no well water). Look to the northwest for the plume from the smelter in Flin Flon. The vegetation briefly resembles northern muskeg as you enter Grass River Provincial Park, but the road rises, and the lusher deciduous forest reappears. Soon after is the junction with PTH 39.

If you are going to Flin Flon, keep straight north on PTH 10, towards Cranberry Portage (full facilities). These 16 km of road are possibly the flattest and straightest of the northern trip, but the promise of better topography is on the horizon. The 51 km from Cranberry Portage to Flin Flon are exciting riding. The Canadian Shield thrusts to the surface and the road narrows. Contend with steep climbs, fast descents, and speeding ore trucks. The scenery is starkly beautiful and northern, with jumbles of rocks, and lakes and conifers. Explore and rest in any of the six wayside parks along the way, especially at Bakers Narrows, where the road bumps up against the jagged bays of Athapapuskow Lake. A viewing tower just inside the park gives you a different perspective on both the scenery and the local history of resource extraction. Flin Flon (full facilities) remains a mining town today, built on sheer rock, and shadowed by the smelter.

Further south at the junction of highways 39 and 10, an eastward turn takes you into the beautiful scenery of Grass River Provincial Park with its many crystal blue lakes. Simonhouse and Reed Lakes are exquisite, and long and overnight stops are recommended at both. Swim, fish, or laze about in a canoe or on the shore.

On the road through the park, fractured dolomite bedrock pops up in several places. As you leave the park and approach Wekusko Lake, Precambrian bedrock briefly adds higher hills. The quality of the road deteriorates in this section. The many ditches cleared perpendicular to the road are an attempt to reduce the ice-heaving stress of poor drainage.

The trip north (left) on PR 392 to Wekusko Falls is worthwhile. Enjoy the twisting, hilly road, glowing with an unusual pink hue. Although wide and in good repair, the route is heavily traveled by ore trucks. Wekusko Falls (full facilities) is a series of cascades on the Grass River, spanned by several walking bridges. A further 17 km north is the end of the road at Snow Lake (full facilities).

Continuing east on PTH 39 past the last picnic site on Wekusko Lake, the trees grade into stunted spruces. The return train to The Pas or Winnipeg can be caught in two locations: at Wekusko, 8 km down a gravel road; or 45 km further east at Ponton, the junction with PTH 6.

Day Rides and Tour Extensions

A very challenging alternative to these touring options is to ride much of this northern landscape while participating in the annual Northern Cycle Tour. 'Tour' has a different meaning for the event organizers: the full distance of 210 km between Snow Lake and The Pas is ridden in one day! A metric century (100 km), and a family ride of 40 km are also included. All rides are one way, and the starts are staggered, so that riders from all three distances converge near the end. Obtain further details from the Kelsey Recreation Centre office in The Pas.

Consider extending the tour to Thompson (camping or accommodation are too far flung to allow cycle-touring on PTH 6 south to the Interlake region). From Ponton to Wabowden (47 km), the terrain is flat, the trees are stunted and the road is straight and heavily traveled. However, northeast of Wabowden beautiful lakes reappear, Manitoba's largest waterfall gushes, and in the vicinity of Paint Lake the hills and tall trees return again. Avoid the Ponton-to-Wabowden drudgery by connecting via bus from Snow Lake or Ponton to Wabowden. Ride the 106 km from Waboden to Thompson, with an overnight stop mandatory in beautiful Paint Lake Provincial Recreation Park (83 km from Wabowden; camping, lodge and restaurant facilities).

The Northern Parks Tour can also be extended from a southerly direction. PTH 10 originates in the Turtle Mountains on the American border. Long-distance enthusiasts could begin there, pedal north to Wasagaming, and then ride the Northern Parks Tour to Flin Flon or Thompson. The Mouse and Turtle Tour (p.36) covers PTH 10 from the border to Brandon. The segment from Brandon to Wasagaming (100 km) would be a challenging uphill ride. It could be broken in Minnedosa (42 km from Brandon; full facilities). Averaging approximately 100 km per day, this is an 11+ day adventure.

With a mountain bike, more cycling possibilities open up. Along the southern half of the tour, explore the trails of Riding Mountain National Park (p.154), Duck Mountain Provincial Park (p.133), and the Roaring River Canyon (p.163). Ride the ski trails at Clearwater Lake Provincial Park for hilly challenges in the north, or investigate the back roads south of Cranberry Portage (p.145).

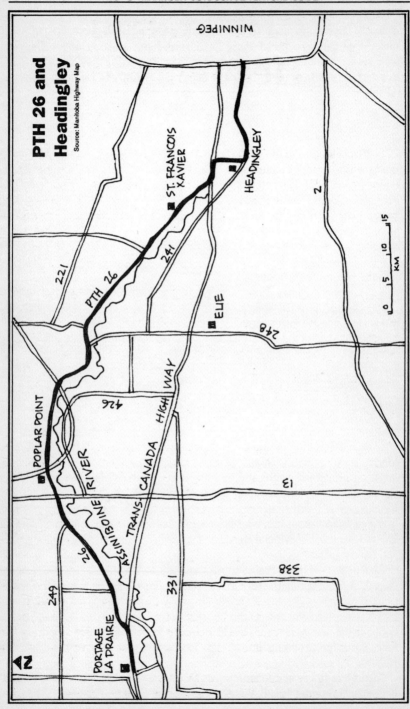

PTH 26 and Headingley

Source: Manitoba Highway Map

PTH 26 and Headlingley

PTH 26 is a section of the old Trans-Canada Highway in central Manitoba. It is a beautiful road, gracefully curving with the riverbank forest of the Assiniboine River. PTH 26 stretches for 64 km between Portage la Prairie and St. Francois Xavier. Winnipeg is a further 17 km to the east, and the best cycling connection is via Headingley and PR 241. This route serves many functions: it is a well-known training and recreational day ride; it can be part of an overnight tour; or a return trip qualifies as a century (100 miles) ride.

Type: Paved road day rides or tours.
Access: Begin in either Winnipeg or Portage la Prairie. In Winnipeg consult the Cyclist's Map of Winnipeg to find the best route to the Perimeter Highway where Roblin Boulevard becomes PR 241. In Portage la Prairie, ride to the eastern end of the city along Highway 1A to connect with PTH 26.
Facilities: Full facilities in Winnipeg and Portage. Stores and snacks in Headingley, St. Francois Xavier and Poplar Point.
Distance: From Perimeter in Winnipeg to Portage is 83 km one way; Winnipeg to Headingley is 16 km return.
Difficulty: Easy to moderate (easy to difficult distance; easy hills).

The route to Headingley and back is a pleasant day ride from Winnipeg. Across the Perimeter at Roblin Road the landscape is suddenly rural, with numerous market gardens and a golf course among the cultivated fields. The road swings northward just before crossing the Assiniboine River. Turn west (left) into Headingley, and ride to where the pavement ends before retracing your tracks to the city. On a mountain bike or a touring bike you could continue a further 2 km to Beaudry Provincial Heritage Park, where you can stroll among elms and basswoods.

To ride to Portage la Prairie from Winnipeg, follow PR 241 north across the river, instead of taking the turn to Headingley. Turn west (left) onto the Trans-Canada Highway, and briefly brave the heavy car and semi-trailer traffic. Just past the weigh station swing onto the service road running parallel to the north. Look for the plaque marking the Principal Meridian. If you are on a mountain bike, consider dropping into North Beaudry for some riverside cruising (p.121).

The white horse statue announces St. Francois Xavier and the turn north (right; 10 km) onto PTH 26. Wander this route and enjoy. The trees, the towns, and the curves provide dimension and interest to an otherwise flat ride through an agricultural plain. Poplar Point is reached after 40 km. Close to Portage is St. Annes's Church, the oldest log church in Western Canada. Stop in to observe its austere style and the historic graveyard graced by spreading elms. After the church the trees melt away, and for the last kilometers grain fields, vegetable rows and the big sky dominate the view. PTH 26 joins Highway 1A just east of Portage.

This route can be a tour from Winnipeg if you stay overnight in Portage la Prairie (or vice-versa), and return the same way the next day. The Winnipeg Cycletouring Club uses this route as a century ride. To put in 100 miles, ride from the Park West Hotel on Roblin Boulevard near the Perimeter, along the route described above, to Crescent Lake in Portage la Prairie, then turn around and crank those pedals all the way back. Congratulations!

PTH 31 to Windygates

This route may at first seem like a long ride to nowhere, but it includes some of the toughest paved climbs in the province, and certainly in proximity to Winnipeg. The sharp, deep valley of the Pembina River in southcentral Manitoba provides the challenge. PTH 31 is so challenging that the Manitoba Cycling Association uses it for races. Non-racers can also pit themselves against the valley walls. While not exactly a family ride, the route becomes a day excursion when combined with lunch in Maida, the American town across from Windygates known for its restaurants.

Type: Paved road day rides.
Access: Begin and end at Darlingford on PTH 3, or at La Verendrye wayside park at junction of PTHs 31 and 3.
Facilities: Full facilities at Darlingford; restaurants across border in Maida; no more along route.
Distance: 22 km one-way to Windygates.
Difficulty: Moderate to difficult (moderate distance; difficult hills).

For the first 5 km, PTH 31 is innocently flat, crossing open croplands. Dip once, then climb, dip again and then climb for just under 2 km. There is a final stretch of flat land, then hang on for the fast, electrifying drop of 90 m to the Pembina River. Grab a glance down the wooded valley without losing momentum for the hill ahead. The climb up and out is in two stages: a moderate puff to a brief terrace, then the final steep grunt. Cresting the top, the road points straight south across mildly undulating fields all the way to the one-house border crossing at Windygates.

To return, wheel around and do it all over again. This time the downhill is gentler, but the ascent is steeper and continuously demanding. If you're riding a mountain bike or a solid touring bike, consider connecting with the Pembina Valley gravel roads described on p.91.

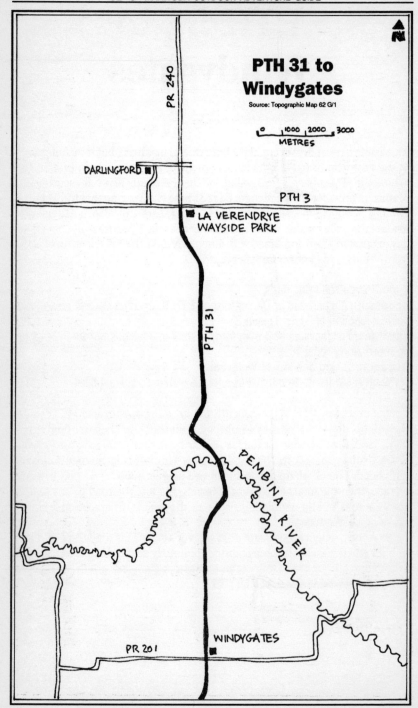

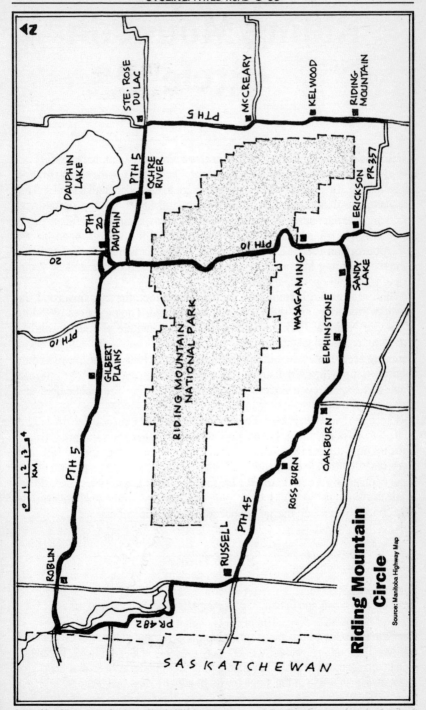

Riding Mountain
Circle

Source: Manitoba Highway Map

Riding Mountain Circle

A boreal island in Manitoba's agricultural sea, Riding Mountain National Park sits grandly atop the Manitoba Escarpment. Slicing northwestwards through the province, the escarpment marks a change in elevation, and a switch from flat plains to rolling parkland terrain. Charm and variety are the signature of this tour. There are spruce forests and aspen groves, grain fields and pastures, flat road and terrifying hills, thriving rural communities and wide open spaces. One route option also takes you through Asessippi Provincial Park, the virtual opposite of Riding Mountain National Park. Small and dominated by water, Asessippi is more prairie than parkland.

This cycle touring is among the best in the province: the roads are good, the traffic is moderate, and the scenery is sensational. The pleasures of Riding Mountain National Park and its environs also include abundant wildlife, excellent recreational attractions, and frequent towns with full facilities. Camping accentuates the outdoor pleasures of this tour, although with some modifications to the daily distances, fast-and-light touring is possible. Intermediate and expert cycletourers will particularly enjoy the challenges and pleasures of this trip.

There are two main routes. The first tour covers 241 km in three days. This route travels north along the plain, skirting the edge of the escarpment, then hops up onto it near Dauphin, and returns southward through the hills and trees of the park. A five day tour circles the park to the south, west and north, before traversing it back to the starting point. A strong cyclist could condense this into a four day trip. This longer route is highly recommended for its variety of scenery and a much higher proportion of hills and curves.

Short Tour

Type: Paved road tours.
Access: Start and end in hamlet of Riding Mountain or Kelwood, on PTH 5, north of Neepawa.
Facilities: Moderate distances between towns, except in Riding Mountain National Park, where full facilities are only available in Wasagaming. Frequent picnic and camping areas with water throughout the park. Note that no facilities are available in the small towns of either Riding Mountain or Kelwood.

Distance: Total 241 km suggested as follows:

day 1- Riding Mountain to Dauphin	103 km
day 2- Dauphin to Lake Katherine	65 km
day 3- Lake Katherine to Riding Mountain	73 km

Difficulty: Moderate (moderate distance; moderate to difficult hills).

For the initial 60 km along PTH 5, the road is basically straight and flat, with only gradual hills and turns. But the view to the left keeps changing as the escarpment wall pushes upward to the west and the north. From the hamlet of Riding Mountain north, all fields have disappeared from the folds and crests, and the escarpment rises steeply, thickly covered with forests. Further north at McCreary, the sharp face recedes to the west, and the land opens up again to grain and canola fields. This is the low lying land of the Turtle River, which drains past Ste. Rose du Lac into Lake Dauphin.

Ste. Rose du Lac is a pleasant farm community (60 km; full facilities). PTH 5 shifts westward (left) after Ste. Rose, still skirting the prominent silhouette of Riding Mountain. Turn north (right) onto PTH 20, which leads to Rainbow Beach Provincial Recreation Park (6 km; swimming and camping), then carries on to Dauphin (18 km; full facilities).

Head south from Dauphin on PTH 10. Just beyond the junction of PTH 5 is the site of the annual Selo Ukrainia or the Ukrainian Festival, usually held around the July long weekend. Soon after, enter Riding Mountain National Park (16 km; pick up the excellent park maps at the gate),and begin the climb up the escarpment. It's a long, slow and brutal ascent, but half way up waits a picnic area and a viewing tower with a great panorama to the north.

Once the Escarpment is crested, rolling hills dominate the topography. There is a paved shoulder, and the speed limit is 80 km/hr, so settle in and enjoy the 46 km to Lake Katherine. PTH 10 crosses two of the three main environments found in Riding Mountain National Park: the northern boreal forest, and the eastern hardwood forest. There are several opportunities to stop and relax, and to take a closer look at the wilderness. Explore Moon Lake, the Bead Lakes Trail and the Boreal Island Self-guiding Trail. More aspen and white spruce, a fast descent, and the road is at the shores of Clear Lake. Follow the hills to the junction with PR 19. This part gravel, part paved road leads to the Lake Katherine campground (3 km from the junction) as well as to several good hiking trails. Alternate accommodation in Wasagaming (full facilities).

There are two approaches to Wasagaming: continue on PTH 10 to the signposted junction, or follow cottage roads along the shores of Clear Lake. Access to this scenic and less traveled route is just after the magnificent downhill by the golf course. Admire the lake and grunt up the hill, turning west (right) at Wasagaming Drive. There is a scenic lookout and a lakeshore hike along the ride into the town.

Leaving Wasagaming and Riding Mountain National Park, climb up to Onanole, then follow the dips and bends of PTH 10 through to Erickson (20 km; full facilities except camping). On the hill south of town, turn east (left) onto PR 357, sometimes referred to as Mountain Road (actually the name of a village). Riding this rollicking road with good views to the north and the south is a wonderful end to the tour, especially the exhilarating descent to PTH 5. Nip north (left) along this highway to the starting point at Riding Mountain or Kelwood.

Long Tour

Type: Paved road tours.
Access: Depending on the alternative selected, start and end in either Sandy Lake on PTH 45 west of Erickson, or in Wasagaming in Riding Mountain National Park.
Facilities: Frequent towns, most with full facilities. Several B&B in area. Riding Mountain has frequent picnic and camping sites, but full facilities only in Wasagaming.
Distance: Two itineraries for a total tour of 366 km (or 392 with camping at Rossman Lake) suggested as follows:
Alternative I

day 1- Sandy Lake to Russell	89 km
day 2- Russell to Roblin Kin Park	83 km
day 3- Roblin to Gilbert Plains	63 km
day 4- Gilbert Plains to Moon Lake	63 km
day 5- Moon Lake to Sandy Lake	68 km

Alternative II

day 1- Wasagaming to Rossman Lake	97 km
day 2- Rossman Lake to Asessippi	82 km
day 3- Asessippi to Grandview	99 km
day 4- Grandview to Wasagaming	115 km

Difficulty: Moderate to difficult (distance and hills).

Whether you start in Wasagaming or Sandy Lake, the first day's ride sets the pace for the tour. From the junction of PTH 10, PTH 45 is exciting riding, with rapidly rolling hills and steep river valleys. Many lakes are visible through the trees and fields. From Sandy Lake (27 km from Wasagaming; full facilities) zip up and down a few more hills and there is Elphinstone, tucked among the folds of the Little Saskatchewan River valley. It's a fast ride down, and an equally steep climb up the other side of the valley.

West from Elphinstone the hills moderate, although the road continues to wind. On this quasi-plateau, the trees diminish and the view opens up, with mixed agricultural land all the way to Russell. At Rossburn (54 km; full facilities), PR 577 travels north (right) then east (right) to Rossman Lake, and overnight camping (13 km). West of Rossburn on PTH 45, the Birdtail Creek cuts a wide and deep notch through the landscape.

At Russell (50 km; full facilities) turn north (right) on PTH 83. Slowly a good view evolves to the west along this flat, straight road, as the valley of the Assiniboine River drops away. There are some good descents and slight climbs before reaching the junction with PR 482 (19 km). Turn west (left) and follow PR 482 for 13 km before it plunges down to the Shellmouth dam and Asessippi Provincial Park. Relax in this serene park with excellent camping and recreational facilities, well worth an extended visit.

Cycling PR 482 from Asessippi Provincial Park is one of the highlights of this trip. It is a little-traveled route that affords superb views of the long Assiniboine River reservoir called Lake of the Prairies. There are three sets of climbs or descents guaranteed to eliminate any grumbles about flat Manitoba. There are two wayside parks set a few kilometers down gravel roads. At the junction with PTH 5, turn east (right; 37 km) to swoop down and across the Lake of the Prairies. Camping is found along its eastern shore.

Cycling east on PTH 5 from Roblin (13 km; full facilities), a series of rivers and creeks have carved a succession of hills. The valley of the Shell River is particularly picturesque and steep. The land levels on the trek eastward through Grandview (48 km) and Gilbert Plains (15 km from Grandview; both full facilities). Dauphin (30 km; full facilities) can be bypassed by swinging south on PTH 5 and 10. Continue south on PTH 10 to the park entrance.

The last leg of the tour is through the wild beauty of Riding Mountain National Park. The trip through the park along PTH 10 has been described above. It's hilly, it's undeveloped and it's beautiful. South of the park, the hills carry you back to the junction with PTH 45.

Day Rides and Tour Extensions

The entire parkland region excels in day rides. Three are particularly recommended. PR 382 along the Lake of the Prairies and PR 357 through Mountain Road vie for the best scenery and the steepest hills. The few paved roads in Riding Mountain National Park all offer superb day rides. Cruise the cottage roads of Wasagaming and along the north shore of Clear Lake.

Touring through Riding Mountain National Park is included in the Northern Parks Tour (p.41). The Riding Mountain Circle could also be extended by riding south on PTH 10 to Brandon (100 km), then connecting with the Mouse and Turtle Tour (p.36).

If your bike can handle gravel roads, even more cycling awaits you. Explore PTH 19 and the Audy Lake Road within Riding Mountain National Park, or investigate the network of gravel roads south of the park (p.101). Further south, there is a hilly gravel road tour near Rivers (p.81).

Last but not least, Riding Mountain National Park offers one of the most extensive networks of off road trails in the province, ranging from easy day trips to mountain bike camping (p.154).

The Road to Hecla

Endless beaches and a stunning provincial park are the key attractions of this tour, which stretches northward through the Interlake region of Manitoba to Hecla Island. The suggested route maximizes waterfront views, beginning with roads alongside the Red River, and continuing with those roads closest to Lake Winnipeg. The tour culminates in Hecla Island Provincial Park. The park encompasses over a dozen islands and rocks, a wildlife refuge, a historic village, and a developed resort and recreation area. This is a superb summertime ride, when a holiday atmosphere reigns in the series of beach resorts along the lake.

The road to Hecla is a good route for beginning and expert cyclists alike. The frequent facilities allow daily distances to be chosen to suit most abilities. However, there are a few detractions to consider. The roads are straight and flat, and if a strong wind blows against you it is a long, tough haul with no relief. Cyclists must also be prepared for heavy summer traffic and for short segments of gravel road. Lower summer speed limits and planned bike paths in the Gimli area will alleviate some of the traffic problems. The final few km to Gull Harbor are still gravel at the time of writing, but are expected to be paved by 1991.

The route from Winnipeg to Gull Harbor on Hecla Island is described below. The tour could be started in several other locations, such as Gimli or any of the cottage towns. Day rides are pleasurable along all segments of the route.

Type: Paved road tours and day rides.

Access: Tour could start and end anywhere along route from Winnipeg to Hecla. Consult the Cyclist's Map of Winnipeg to find the best access to one of the three routes out of the city: Henderson Highway, Main St., or McPhillips St. Return along the same route, catch a bus in Riverton, or arrange pick-up.

Facilities: Frequent towns with partial or full facilities along most of the route. Riverton is the last town with full facilities before Gull Harbor.

Distance: Several daily distances can be selected. Two suggested one way routes are as follows:

Alternative I

day 1- Winnipeg to Winnipeg Beach	66 km
day 2- Winnipeg Beach to Hnausa	46 km
day 3- Hnausa to Gull Harbor	63 km

Alternative II

day 1- Winnipeg to Gimli	82 km

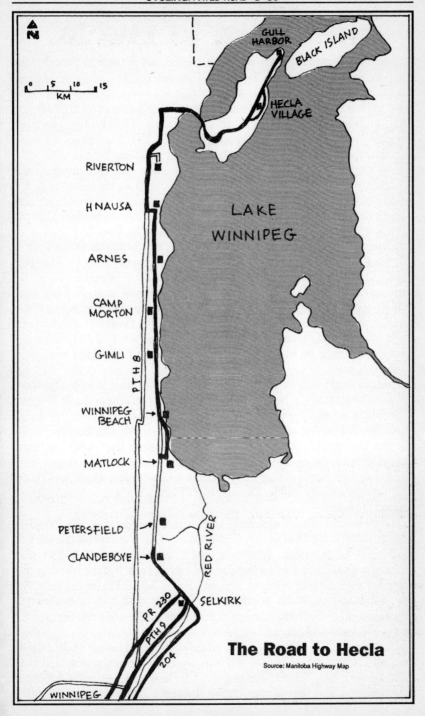

The Road to Hecla

Source: Manitoba Highway Map

day 2- Gimli to Gull Harbor   93 km
Difficulty: Easy to moderate (easy to moderate distance; easy hills).

Beginning in Winnipeg, there are three choices in the route to Selkirk. The most scenic routes are either Henderson Highway (PR 204) along the eastern bank of the Red River (p.26), or PTH 9 (Main St.) north, turning off at River Road and following this historic route to where it rejoins the main highway just south of Selkirk (p.95; road surface oiled gravel). The shortest but most heavily traveled routes out of Winnipeg are either PTH 9 to Selkirk (20 km), or PTH 8 (McPhillips St.) north, swinging onto PR 230 to Selkirk (24 km).

There are two choices from Selkirk. Either follow the more direct PTH 9 northwestward past Clandeboye (10 km), or detour along the more scenic PR 320 (p.87), turning west (left) to Clandeboye. This choice is longer by 9 km and is partly along gravel roads. The section from Clandeboye to Matlock (22 km) traverses the western edge of the extensive Netley Marshes.

Turn east (right) on PR 232 to reach Matlock, and the first beaches. Follow 232 along the shore through successive cottage communities to Winnipeg Beach. There are numerous stores and restaurants or concessions along the route and in Winnipeg Beach. Rejoin PTH 9 to continue northward to Gimli. This stretch is dominated by cottages, but there are many good glimpses of the lake. Gimli (15 km from Winnipeg Beach; full facilities) is well known for both its Icelandic heritage, and for its miles of sand beaches. Get into the Viking spirit by attending the annual festival in August, or by a visit to the wharf-side museum.

Ride north of Gimli on PR 222. This section of the route is very attractive, and the cottage traffic tapers off. Admire the 8 km segment to Camp Morton, where the road winds through the thick forests protected by the provincial park. The fall colors are spectacular here. Investigate the Heritage Park opposite the hamlet of Camp Morton, and picnic along the lakeshore. From Camp Morton to Arnes (10 km; full facilities), the road is lined with aspen, ash, elm and spruce. North of Arnes, the road curves back to the shore, and Hecla Island becomes fully visible. Picnic, swim or camp at the provincial park at Hnausa (14 km).

Follow the paved road west (left) of Hnausa to the junction with PTH 8. It is 11 km to the turnoff to Riverton (full facilities). This pleasant town is the last opportunity for provisions before the final 52 km to Gull Harbor. To reach Hecla, the road takes a sweeping curve north and east before crossing the causeway over Grassy Narrows and into Hecla Island Provincial Park. An extensive marsh covers the southwestern tip (accessible by boardwalk); it is a staging area for thousands of migrant ducks and geese, and breeding ground for grebes, terns and herons.

After passing the park gate, the road cuts across the center of the island, through the vegetation typical of Hecla: swampy spruce stands and rich deciduous growths. Watch for members of the large moose population. Road improvements and paving are routing the main highway away from the shoreline, but choose the turnoff to the east (right) towards Hecla Village. The road curves northward along the shore, and while there are patches of gravel, this is the best scenery of the tour. There is a maritime feel here as the wind brings the odor of fish, and gulls reel overhead. The forests of Black Island and the eastern shore of Lake Winnipeg are clearly visible, and to the north a lighthouse glints. Several of the fishermen's houses still remain in use, trim yellow and white frame structures staring over the water. Hecla Village is well worth a visit; stroll along the self-guiding trail for insights into this Icelandic fishing village (store and B&B).

From Hecla Village it is a short 9 km to Gull Harbor and the end of the tour. Camping and resort accommodations are available, among extensive recreational facilities, including beaches, hiking trails and a golf course. If you ride a mountain bike here, explore Hecla Island further along the back roads and trails described on p.139.

Rock Lake Tour

A delightful weekend trip of moderate difficulty, the Rock Lake Tour explores the pleasant rolling countryside of southcentral Manitoba. The tour starts above the broad, deep valley of the Pembina River, then turns to dip in and out of the steep valley walls three times. The roads are straight, but there is frequent variety in the hummocky hills and the sweeping views. A wonderful weekend run for accomplished cycletourers, the Rock Lake Tour also allows less experienced cyclists to try longer distances and a few stiff hills. Ride this in the summertime, and splash in Rock Lake and Killarney Lake in the evenings.

With the exception of PTH 3, traffic levels are light, and all roads are in good condition. Camp or travel fast-and-light (begin the latter from overnight accommodation in Pilot Mound, Crystal City or La Riviere; 21, 26, and 43 extra km respectively).

Type: Paved road tours.
Access: Tour begins and ends at the north shore campgrounds of Rock Lake, along PR 253 in southcentral Manitoba.
Facilities: Towns with partial or full facilities at moderate distances: scarcest in the Rock Lake area at the start and end of the tour. Carry sufficient water and snacks. Reservations for all accommodation recommended for Killarney during summer weekends.
Distance: Total tour distance of 161 km as follows:
      day 1- Rock Lake to Killarney   87 km
      day 2- Killarney to Rock Lake   74 km
Difficulty: Moderate (distances and hills).

Nestled in soft, enclosing hills, Rock Lake is a charming start to the tour. Ride onto PR 253 as it travels north then west above Rock Lake and the Pembina Valley. Near the village of Glenora (7 km; no facilities) a vast panorama of the wide open, rolling terrain appears. Gently descend to the junction with PTH 5. Cycle north (right) across the uneven deposits of glacial moraine, cut by the occasional stream, then turn west (left) onto PTH 23. The undulations continue, with an overall but slight climb, as you skirt the southern edge of the Tiger Hills and pedal past Belmont (39 km; picnic and restaurant). Just before Ninette, the road swoops back into the Pembina Valley. It's a long, exciting curve down, past the former tuberculosis sanatorium to the shores of Pelican Lake.

Rest and get refreshed in Ninette (16 km; full facilities). Visit the beach at Pelican Lake (sometimes plagued by algal blooms), and the ice cream shop

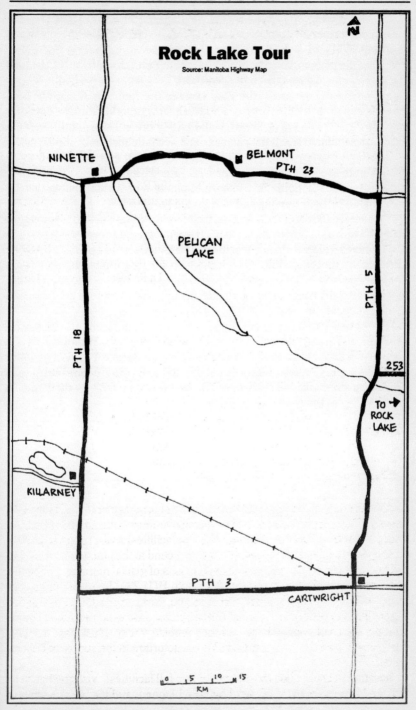

Rock Lake Tour

Source: Manitoba Highway Map

N

NINETTE

BELMONT
PTH 23

PELICAN
LAKE

PTH 5

253

TO →
ROCK
LAKE

PTH 18

KILLARNEY

PTH 3

CARTWRIGHT

0   5   10   15
KM

displaying a composite of the region's topographical maps, where you can count the number of contours crossed. To leave Ninette, follow the joint signs marking PTHs 23 and 18, and grunt up and out of the valley. Soon after reaching the plateau, take the turn to the south (left), down PTH 18. The final leg to Killarney passes through scenic farmland, interspersed with several minor valleys. Once more, the road crosses the Pembina River, but here erosion has shaped the valley into a wide, shallow trough. From the outskirts of Killarney (27 km; full facilities), pedal a few more km straight through the business section to reach the campsite and accommodation by the lake.

Leaving Killarney Lake, join PTH 3 and ride briefly east (left). Turn south (right) onto the joint highways 3 and 18. After 11 km veer east (left) again, staying on PTH 3. Settle in for more kilometers of scenic, rolling terrain, punctuated by both thriving and abandoned homesteads.

Just before Cartwright (35 km; full facilities including a bakery), you return to PTH 5 with a left turn to the north. PTH 5 takes a jagged course back towards the Pembina Valley and the ghost town of Neelin. Oak and aspen flash past on the descent, then it's a slow, difficult climb back up to the plateau. After 24 km the junction with PR 253 is reached, and the loop is complete. Retrace your tire tracks eastward (right turn) up PR 253, through Glenora, and coast back to Rock Lake and the start.

The easiest extension to the Rock Lake Tour is to hook up with the Mouse and Turtle Tour (p.36), which extends west and south. Following PTH 5 further north leads to pleasant pedaling through Spruce Woods Provincial Heritage Park. Consider off road riding in the park (p.175). For gravel road cyclists, a strenuous but rewarding ride beckons from more of the Pembina River Valley to the southeast (p.91).

St. Adolphe and St. Norbert

The ride to St. Adolphe is a popular training ride with the racing set: groups of bright jerseys and churning legs frequently flash by. Its proximity to Winnipeg and the pretty scenery along the curving road also make it attractive to recreational cyclists and families. Traffic levels are moderate, although higher on weekends and along PTH 75. Spring rides are particularly rewarding: south winds push you and migrating hawks home, and there is a chance to see the Winnipeg Floodway in operation.

Type: Paved road day rides.
Access: Ride begins in Winnipeg at the Perimeter Highway, where St. Mary's Road becomes PR 200. Return is to same point or to the junction of PTH 75 (Pembina Highway) and the Perimeter. Consult the Cyclist's Map of Winnipeg to access these points. Parking at Maple Grove Park off St. Mary's Road.
Facilities: Restaurants and shops in St. Adolphe.
Distance: 35 km over flat terrain.
Difficulty: Easy (distances and hills).

Ride to St. Adolphe from the Perimeter Highway along PR 200. The landscape is immediately rural, passing market gardens and rural residences. Crest the overpass for the Floodway, and consider the short detour to the control structure. As the road winds south, grain farms and oak forests mingle around each curve. Rest and refuel in St. Adolphe, a pleasant Franco-Manitoban community. Cyclists looking for extra kilometers can continue past the town, but the road becomes straight, flat, and open.

The return loop crosses the Red River just north of the town. Pedal north (right turn) on PTH 75 for 2.5 km, then take the first road to the east (right), which is Red River Road. A delightful spin, the road follows the bends of the river with several vivid reminders of the river's proximity. In places the road has slumped with the riverbanks, and small dykes protect several houses. Red River Road swings back to the Floodway control structure. Here you can either cross to PR 200 and then return to St. Mary's Road, or you can continue up Red River Road to PTH 75 and the St. Norbert Heritage Park. A ride out of Winnipeg to this commemoration of Métis and Franco-Manitoban culture, and to the Floodway, is a short day trip, although traffic is very heavy on PTH 75.

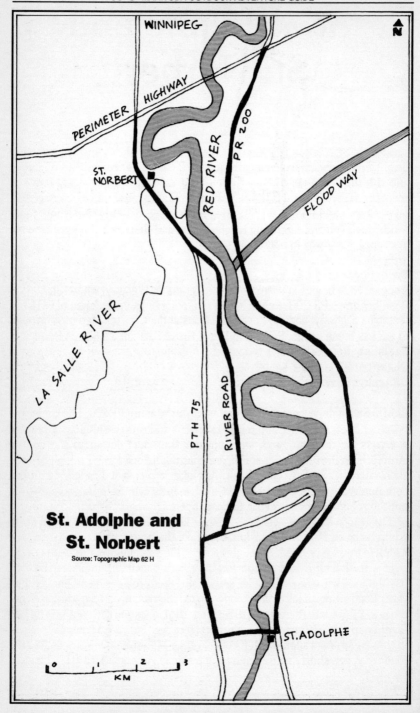

WINNIPEG

PERIMETER HIGHWAY

RED RIVER

PR 200

FLOOD WAY

ST. NORBERT

LA SALLE RIVER

PTH 75

RIVER ROAD

St. Adolphe and
St. Norbert

Source: Topographic Map 62 H

ST. ADOLPHE

N

0 1 2 3
KM

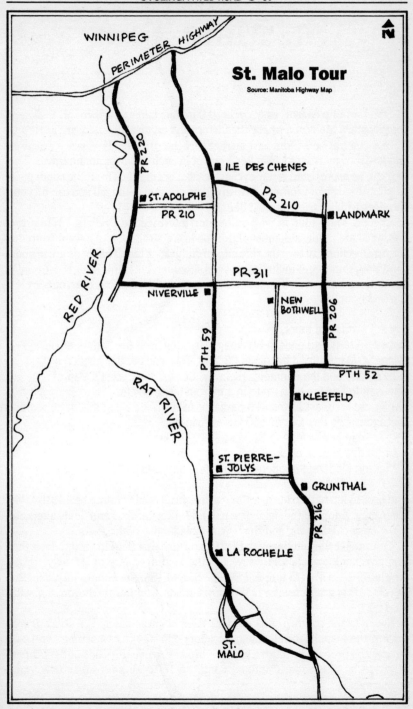

St. Malo Tour

Source: Manitoba Highway Map

St. Malo Tour

In two days of pleasant, easy cycling, this tour takes you through a slice of southeastern Manitoba where the history and cultural diversity are as rich as the agricultural land. Skim past market gardens, grain fields, apiaries, pastures and forests, and rest in a checkerboard of French and Mennonite towns. The tour can be appreciated in any cycling season: warm winds from the south push you home in spring; summer is festival season; and in the fall you can fill your panniers with a varied harvest bounty.

The St. Malo tour is well suited for intermediate cyclists. While the distances are moderate, most of the roads are straight, and a wind from the wrong direction can turn the ride into an endurance test. The roads are in good condition, sometimes including a paved shoulder, but traffic is high, especially on summer weekends. The tour can be cycled with camping gear, or traveled fast-and-light.

Type: Paved road tours.
Access: Starts and ends in Winnipeg. Tour begins at the Perimeter Highway, where St. Mary's Road becomes PR 200. Tour ends at the junction of St. Anne's Road and the Perimeter Highway. Consult the Cyclist's Map of Winnipeg to find the best route to and from these points.
Facilities: Frequent towns with partial or full facilities along the entire route.
Distance: Two day tour of 150 km as follows:

day 1- Winnipeg to St. Malo	70 km
day 2- St. Malo to Winnipeg	80 km

Difficulty: Moderate (moderate distances; easy hills).

The first 15 km of the ride are along a delightful road winding beside the Red River to St. Adolphe (full facilities; p.65). Market gardens and fields alternate with dense oak forests, and the occasional glimpse of the Red.

Continue to the junction with PR 311, and turn east (left) towards Niverville. The riverbank forests fold away, and the land opens up to intensive grain farming. Niverville (15 km; full facilities), a Mennonite community, was the site of the first grain elevator in Western Canada. Continue to the junction with PTH 59.

Swing to the south (right) onto 59. Almost immediately is a short gravel road to the New Bothwell Cheese Factory. On weekday mornings you can peek at the process through a viewing window, while the sales outlet is open through the afternoon. Continue south on PTH 59, past sugar beets and shelterbelts.

Arriving in St. Pierre-Jolys (33 km from Niverville; full services), you are firmly back in Franco-Manitoba. Ease out of the saddle for a while, and investigate La Place des Colons, where a monument and museum celebrate the region's agricultural pioneers.

Pedaling further south, low hills (ancient glacial deposits) metamorphose to the east. To the west, a thick green line draws the course of the Rat River. As you approach St. Malo, hills and river converge, then suddenly the church spires surface, heralding the town (23 km; full facilities). St. Malo Recreation Park is 1.5 km north of the town; this brief ride has the steepest hills of the tour, with a sand beach on the reservoir as the reward.

From St. Malo, ride southwest on PTH 59. The road rises gradually onto the gravel and sand ridge, but the vegetation changes markedly. Fields and pastures disappear, replaced by scrubby oak and aspen forests. Turn north (left) onto PR 216. For the next 35 km you'll be riding northward with the gradual transition from forest back to grain fields.

Up to the Mennonite town of Grunthal, livestock operations fill the view and the nostrils. Grunthal claims the title of provincial dairy capital, and boasts the only zoo in eastern Manitoba (23 km; stores and restaurants). Don't miss the sharp left turn of PR 216 into the main street. Kleefeld (14 km; stores and restaurant) is another historic Mennonite town, now the center of a major honey producing region.

It is a short 2 km from Kleefeld to the intersection with PTH 52. Turn east (right) and ride for 4 km before veering north (left) onto PR 206. For the remainder of the ride, flat fields spread out on either side. At the southern edge of Landmark (15 km; restaurant and stores), turn west (left) onto PR 210 and follow it to the junction with PTH 59. Turn north (right) past Ile Des Chenes (13 km; full facilities just off the main highway). The town reputedly received its name during the 1870 flood, when refuge was found on an oak-topped patch of ground.

Continue to the floodway. On the north side, turn west (left) onto a paved road. Follow it to the T-junction, then turn north (right), and pedal back to the Perimeter Highway at St. Anne's Road and Winnipeg.

Stonewall Starter Tour

The Winnipeg Cycletouring Club devised this weekend tour as a good introduction for beginners to camping-touring. The daily distances are generally short, the topography is level, and the camping facilities are good. Winnipeggers can start and end the tour out of their front doors, and it's easy to take a short-cut back if required. This is a good tour for families, with a lot of attractions and facilities along the route to break up the distance for children. Unfortunately traffic densities are high around Winnipeg.

Type: Paved road tour.
Access: Begins in Winnipeg from Raleigh St.and the Perimeter Highway, returning to the junction of the Perimeter Highway and PR 221 (Inkster Blvd.). Consult the Cyclist's Map of Winnipeg to find the best route to and from these points.
Facilities: Full facilities in Birds Hill Provincial Park (except hotels), Lockport, Selkirk and Stonewall. Frequent restaurants and stores along route, except along PTH 67.
Distance: A three day tour of 93 km as follows (distances from the Perimeter Highway):

day 1- Winnipeg to Birds Hill Park	12 km
day 2- Birds Hill Park to Stonewall	61 km
day 3- Stonewall to Winnipeg	20 km

Difficulty: Easy (distances and hills).

The first leg of the tour is short enough to be ridden on a Friday afternoon or evening. To reach Birds Hill Provincial Park, there are three main choices, which are described in more detail on p.25. One route is Raleigh Road to the Perimeter, then across to the road which parallels first the Perimeter and then PTH 59. Turn east (right) on Camsell Ave., then onto PTH 59. Veer east (right) on PR 213, and north (left) on PR 206 up to the east gate of Birds Hill Provincial Park. At the T-junction after the gate, follow the South Drive (left turn) to the campground.

The second day is the longest, and the distance cycled is comparable to many of the other touring distances in this book. From the campground, retrace your tire tracks to the east gate on PR 206. Turn north (left) and pedal to the junction with PTH 44. Turn west (left) and ride across PTH 59 to the cloverleaf where PR 204 heads north. Consider a detour to the Kenosewin Interpretative Center at Lockport. Kenosewin is a Cree word meaning 'there are many fishes', and the center explains archaeological investigations of the culture of the Larter Indians, who fished the Red River 3,000 years ago.

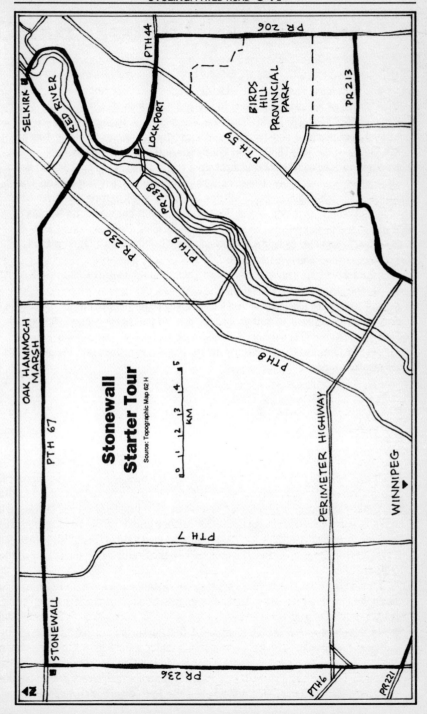

Stonewall Starter Tour

Source: Topographic Map 62 H

PR 204 curves gracefully along the Red River to Selkirk, occasionally bumping up against the bends of the river for scenic views. The long, narrow lots are a remnant from the early days of settlement. Selkirk (12 km from Lockport; full facilities) once vied with Winnipeg for the status of provincial capital, but now claims the title of Catfish Capital of North America. Refuel, rest and relax at Selkirk Park and the Marine Museum of Manitoba.

Ride south of Selkirk on PTH 9 to the junction with PTH 67. Lower Fort Garry National Historic Park stretches along the riverbank just before the junction. Beautifully reconstructed and expertly staffed to replicate the fur trading days of the late 1800s, Fort Garry is another worthy diversion.

To continue the tour, cycle straight west (right turn) on PTH 67 for 35 km. This road seems squarely in agricultural Manitoba, but a stop at the Oak Hammock Marsh is a step back in time to the prairies before the extensive drainage of wetlands in Manitoba. The marsh is well-known for its hordes of migrating ducks, geese, grebes and other waterfowl. Carry on along PTH 67 to Stonewall, and the campground located in the Stonewall Quarry Park, a former limestone quarry with kilns.

The final day of the tour is again short. Cycle straight south of Stonewall on PR 236 to the junction with PTH 6 and the CN tracks. On a summer Sunday you may have to wait for the Prairie Dog Central, the oldest steam locomotive still operating on a mainline, to puff past on its way to Grosse Isle. It's a brief pedal southwest (left) on PTH 6 to the Perimeter Highway. Cycle south (left) on the Perimeter for 3 km to the junction with PR 221. Follow this road (east or left turn) into Winnipeg.

The Whiteshell

Whiteshell Provincial Park in eastern Manitoba has long served as a recreational mecca. Much of the activity focuses on the pristine waterways, but the Whiteshell also has attractions for cyclists. The region really shines as a paved road route. The Whiteshell is the answer for every cyclist driven to despair by flat, straight roads. Look forward to lots of ups and downs, almost continuous curves, and stunning Canadian Shield scenery.

The Whiteshell boasts frequent facilities, ranging from primitive picnic areas to elegant dining and accommodation. Enjoy fast-and-light touring or cycle camping. Combine hiking, horseback riding, swimming and canoeing with cycling for an extended holiday.

The area's popularity also means that a lot of cars are competing with cyclists for the same narrow and potholed strip which forms the one main road through the park. Summer is not the best time to tour the Whiteshell, and cycling on a Friday evening or Sunday afternoon in midsummer is suicidal. Spring and fall are superb seasons in the Whiteshell, however, with the added benefit of cooler temperatures, and either spring flowers or brilliant autumn colors.

Cycling possibilities abound for riders of all abilities. Two routes are described below, which cover most of the Whiteshell region, and day rides and tour extensions are also listed. The best way to enjoy the Whiteshell is a leisurely jaunt, with lots of time to dawdle and enjoy the other park facilities. All levels of cyclists can appreciate this first circle tour. Advanced and intermediate riders can compress the 133 hilly km into 2 days; families and beginning cycletourers can select among the frequent facilities to tailor a tour of virtually any length.

For those who really must ride all the way from Winnipeg, the Whiteshell is accessible by bicycle on a three day tour featuring one easy day sandwiched between two hard days. Consider adding a fourth day in the park, either relaxing, or doing an out-and-back spin along PTH 44 to West Hawk or Falcon Lakes. This second tour is only for fit cyclists. If the wind is blowing in the wrong direction, the long, flat, straight distances make this a grueling endurance test. Regardless, the tour is not highly recommended, because there is more flat prairie grinding than pleasant Whiteshell spinning.

The Whiteshell Circle

Type: Paved road tours.
Access: Suggested tours begin and end in Rennie, just west of the

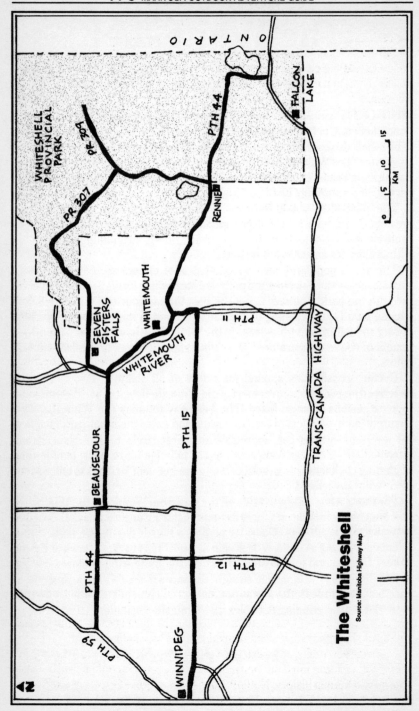

The Whiteshell

Source: Manitoba Highway Map

Whiteshell Provincial Park gate on PTH 44, or at Brereton Lake on PR 307 in the park.

Facilities: Frequent resort areas with full facilities in Whiteshell Provincial Park. Outside the park, only facilities at Seven Sisters Falls, Whitemouth and Rennie. Note that campgrounds and lodges fill up quickly on summer weekends.

Distance: Many tours with different daily distances and destinations could be devised along this route. Two suggestions are:

Alternative I -two day tour:

day 1- Rennie to Otter Falls	57 km
day 2- Otter Falls to Rennie	77 km

Alternative II -three day tour:

day 1- Brereton Lake to Nutimik Lake	36 km
day 2- Nutimik Lake to Whitemouth	54 km
day 3- Whitemouth to Brereton	44 km

Difficulty: Easy to moderate (easy to moderate distance; moderate hills).

To start the tour head east on PTH 44 from Rennie (full facilities). Check the daily goose count at the Alfred Hole Sanctuary, then enter the Whiteshell Provincial Park (pick up the detailed park map). Immediately east of the park entrance, turn north (left) onto PR 307.

North of the railway tracks, Brereton Lake sparkles, the first of the major cottage developments with complete facilities, including two public beaches (4.5 km to the first beach). The road then courses through deciduous forests, crossing the Rennie River twice, before arriving at the shores of Red Rock Lake (18 km). The road now touches two more lakes in quick succession: Jessica Lake and White Lake. A brief detour is recommended at the end of White Lake to view Rainbow Falls (22.5 km; full services).

Immediately beyond White Lake is the junction with PR 309. Cycling to Big Whiteshell Lake and back adds 25 more km of hills and curves. There are a couple of picnic spots along the way, and at the end a developed area with full facilities and a fine sand beach.

Continuing north on PR 307, the road dips across the Whiteshell River, then skirts it again, before curving around Betula Lake (32 km from Rainbow Falls; full services). Just 4.5 km further is the trailhead for the Pine Point Hiking Trail. Consider straying from the saddle to the delightful swimming hole at the rapids.

Less than one km north of the Pine Point trailhead is the petroform display at Bannock Point, although recently the access has not been well marked. The petroforms are ancient Indian rock mosaics in the form of snakes, turtles, fish and birds, but many have been badly damaged by vandals.

More curves, rocks, and trees, and you are upon Nutimik Lake (44.5 km; full services). Visit the museum housed in a log cabin, which depicts the area's natural and human history. Nutimik Lake is actually the first of several bulges and bends in the Winnipeg River. For the next 19 km the road hugs the shoreline, passing many cottages, campgrounds, and lodges in rapid succession. The most westerly stop within the park boundaries is Otter Falls (12.5 km).

Continue westward on PR 307 from Otter Falls around the last few curves on the road before it straightens and traverses dense spruce swamps. The park gate is passed after 6 km, then Seven Sisters Falls is reached after another 10 km. Stop at the picnic grounds and stroll across the sluiceway of the hydroelectric dam.

Leaving Seven Sisters Falls, you zip down to cross the Whitemouth River, a frequent companion for the rest of the ride. At the junction with PTH 11, turn south (left) and follow that highway for a brief 5 km to the junction with PTH 44. Turn southeast (left) and you are on the loop back to Rennie.

The next 20 km or so are delightful riding. While no longer wilderness, the rural scenery is both varied and lovely. The thickly treed and steep banks of the Whitemouth River add a third dimension of depth to the landscape. The community of Whitemouth (16 km, full facilities) just off the main highway is the only source of food and water, unless you add an extra ride down to the small town of Elma.

The landscape begins to change after passing the junction where PTH 11 continues further south. Mixed deciduous and coniferous forest intrudes against the road and fields more frequently. After approximately 5 km you enter Whiteshell Provincial Forest, where the trees really take over. Then suddenly the granite of the Canadian Shield pops through the surface, and you know that you are approaching Rennie and returning to the park.

Winnipeg-Whiteshell Loop

Type: Paved road tours.

Access: The tour starts in Winnipeg at the junction of Lagimodiere Blvd. and PTH 15, at the eastern edge of the city. It finishes in the northeast section of Winnipeg, where PR 204, Henderson Highway, enters the city. Consult the Cyclist's Map of Winnipeg to find the best access to these points.

Facilities: Moderate distances between towns with partial or full facilities on route to and from park. Frequent facilities in Whiteshell Provincial Park.

Distances: A three day tour of 282 km as follows:

day 1- Winnipeg (Perimeter) to Rennie	113 km
day 2- Rennie to Opapiskow Campground	55 km
day 3- Opapiskow Campground to Winnipeg	114 km

Difficulty: Difficult (difficult distances; easy to moderate hills).

To reach the Whiteshell from Winnipeg, the instructions are easy: get onto PTH 15 and ride straight east. From the city's edge to Elma (full facilities except camping) are 75 flat and straight km. The scenery is rural, with a forested interlude as you pass through Agassiz Provincial Forest. At Elma turn north (left) onto PTH 11 for 8 km, then hang a right (southeast) onto PTH 44. You are now onto the route described above. The first camping site is at Rennie, 113 km from Winnipeg's Perimeter Highway.

From Rennie, follow the instructions for the shorter tour, as far as the junction with PTH 44. Turn west (right) at this point, then pump and glide through Agassiz Provincial Forest, down the hill past Seddons Corner, through Beausejour, and all the way to Lockport. Select PR 204 to meander south along the river to Winnipeg (p.26; see also Forest and Falls Tour, p.29).

Day Rides and Tour Extensions

Consider Whiteshell Provincial Park for training or recreational day rides. Start anywhere in the park for a rewarding ride. Particularly recommended are riding east then south on PR 307 from Otter Falls, riding north on PRs 307 and 309 from Brereton Lake to Big Whiteshell (54 km return), or cruising highways 44 and 312 from West Hawk Lake.

The Whiteshell Tour can be extended by connecting with the Forest and Falls Tour (p.29). Cycle more kilometers with off road riding in the Whiteshell (p.187) or in Agassiz Provincial Forest (p.115).

Extended Touring Across Manitoba

Two weeks on a bike around Manitoba? Ride the province north to south? East to west? Manitoba's size and geographical variety open great possibilities for extended bicycle touring, whether the objective is to set new time and distance records, or to leisurely explore the province's attractions. Cyclists crossing Canada need no longer see Manitoba as a flat obstacle, but can fill a route with trees, hills, lakes and rivers.

Most of the routes listed in this book are two to five day tours, with the exception of the complete Northern Parks Tour. Several of the shorter tours could be combined for days or weeks of delightful pedaling. Concentrate on a corner of Manitoba, or span the vast beauty of the province. Several suggestions are offered below, but a tour of virtually any length could be devised.

In eastern Manitoba the Whiteshell Tour and the Forest and Falls Tour (p.73 and p.29) fit together naturally. Begin in Rennie, cycle the Whiteshell on PR 307, follow PTH 11 and the Forest and Falls Tour 'backwards' to Beausejour, then return to Rennie on PTH 44.

For a waterside extravaganza, link the Whiteshell and Forest and Falls Tours with the Road to Hecla (p.58). Begin as above, but at Beausejour ride east on PTH 44 through Lockport to join PTH 9 and the route north to the beaches of Lake Winnipeg. Strong cyclists could ride to Hecla in 5 or 6 days. Enjoy the extensive recreational facilities at a more leisurely pace.

The cycling connections seem endless in southwestern Manitoba. The Rock Lake and the Mouse and Turtle Tours (p.62 and p.36) combine easily. Extend these tours northward to Spruce Woods Provincial Heritage Park. Ride east to the Pembina Hills along PTH 3, with an extra nose-dive into the Pembina Valley at La Riviere. Unfortunately there are few services along PTH 23, and an eastern circle route is hard to devise. With a sturdy touring bike or a mountain bike, add the gravel road pleasures and challenges of the southern Pembina Valley (p.91).

The tours of the southwest can easily be combined with the rolling roads in the parkland region of western Manitoba. Continue north on PTH 10 from the Mouse and Turtle Tour through the deep valley at Minnedosa, to hook up to the Riding Mountain Circle (p.54). Discover the delights of the gravel road network immediately south of Riding Mountain National Park (p.101), or experiment with some of the paved roads northwest of Brandon.

One of the most challenging tours in the province is to cycle from Turtle Mountain to Thompson, starting at the American border, and ending well above the 55th parallel. Start with the Mouse and Turtle Tour (p.36), ride north from Brandon to Wasagaming on PTH 10, then follow the Northern Parks Tour (p.41). Averaging 100 km a day, this is an 11+ day adventure, longer with rest days or shorter daily distances.

Riding east to west (or vice-versa) across Manitoba is a rewarding tour. There are numerous possibilities; for example, you could ride directly into the setting sun or cut diagonally from Roblin or the The Pas to the very southeastern tip at North West Angle.

Creatively combining off road riding or gravel road exploration with paved road tours further expands the possible duration and variety of a Manitoba cycling holiday. Off road riding suggestions are provided in the text of the different paved road tours; also check the off road route summary (p.112) against your planned tour.

As important as deciding where to go is knowing where to avoid. The Trans-Canada Highway (Highway 1) and the Yellowhead Route (PTH 16) are the busiest highways in the province, especially in the summer. Although the Trans-Canada offers double lane, divided highway across much of Manitoba, it crosses the flattest parts of the province, bypassing the best scenery. The Yellowhead is more scenic, but the heavy traffic is funneled along a narrow road. Frequently a scenic alternative parallels the busy highway, such as PTH 2 along the Trans-Canada and PTH 45 along the Yellowhead. Minimize your time spent on the pancake-flat portions of the province, which lie in the Red River Valley (stretching the width between Carman and Steinbach), and in the Interlake. PTH 26 is the best route in to Winnipeg from the west, while from the east, the best approaches are those further north, such as PTH 44.

Planning an extended tour requires preparation, especially to ensure that accommodation is available within acceptable distances. Getting to the start or getting home from the finish of a one-way tour also requires planning. Check bus, train and plane schedules, or arrange drop-off and pick-up by car. Whatever your final choice, enjoy your Manitoba cycling holiday.

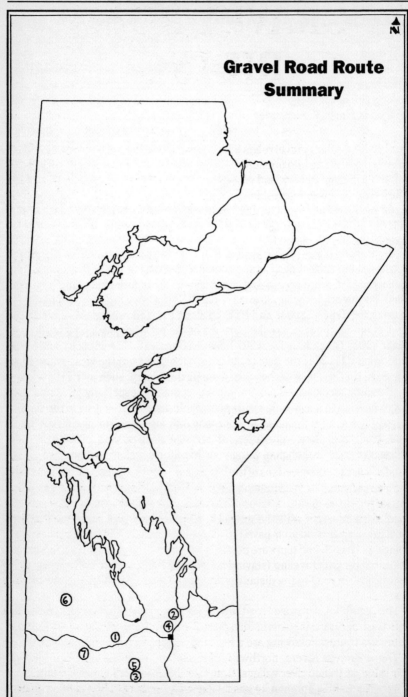

Gravel Road Route Summary

GRAVEL ROAD RIDING

Cycling Manitoba's gravel roads adds a new dimension to the province and to the sport. Reaching into unusual corners of Manitoba, gravel roads offer little traffic, surprising scenery, and enough variety to fill years of cycling. Mountain bikes have renewed interest in cycling these roads, although sturdy touring bikes manage well too. Cycling gravel roads leads you down steep river valleys, up into remote forests, past hamlets and ghost towns, and into kilometers of exploration.

While the advantages of gravel road riding are great, remember three disadvantages: dust, stone chips and limited facilities. Dust or flying stones may keep you off popular gravel roads leading to weekend cottage or recreation areas, but the infrequency of facilities is a more important consideration, and limits touring options. As with paved and off road trips, be prepared when you venture down gravel roads, especially when exploring new areas. Always carry water, food, maps and tools.

In this book, gravel roads refer to numbered Provincial Roads, or good municipal roads allowing fast spinning, most of which are outside of crown land. The Off Road section includes numerous easy-riding back roads, but most of these are not graveled or maintained, and are found in provincial parks, forests, and wildlife management areas. Review the selections in that section, as well as the seven routes or areas described in detail here.

Day rides and tours along gravel roads are described, and are structured similarly to the other sections of the book (see 'How to Use this Book' p.7). Use the overview map or the summary table (p.83) to find interesting rides, or skim the selections to garner a flavor of the area. Some paved road routes and off road rides intersect with the gravel road selections. Mix and match riding surfaces, and expand your paved road or off road repertoire with gravel road spinning. Gravel road tours are possible with camping gear, and in a few cases by 'fast-and-light' traveling (staying at hotels or B&B, and carrying less gear). As with paved road tours, distances and facilities are noted for the few towns passed.

The possibilities of gravel road riding in Manitoba are limitless. Experiment with the rides described here, then discover the fun and satisfaction of finding your own routes. Following are a few suggestions to whet your appetite.

The area near Rivers, northwest of Brandon, provides hills from glacial morraine and steep river valleys. Consider day rides and, possibly, tours.

The Tiger Hills, hummocky glacial deposits south of PTH 2, invite exploration. Day trips could start from Holland or Glenboro, although facilities are infrequent for touring. Connect with the Lavenham area (p.85) or the Treesbank Circuit (p.105).

Many gravel roads radiate from Duck Mountain, and two Provincial Roads slice through the park (p.133). Use the park as a base for day rides, or evaluate tour options, although facilities in the area are limited.

Much of the Interlake region is flat and filled with low trees, but gravel roads mimic the historic Fairford Trail winding near the shores of Lake Manitoba. Start at Watchorn Provincial Recreation Park and cruise north, keeping as far west as possible. Pass through Steep Rock with its limestone cliffs, and end near Fairford on PTH 6.

Include the rocks and trees of the Canadian Shield north of the Winnipeg River in a long tour for experienced cyclists which loops north through Nopiming Provincial Park, turns west along the Wanipigow River system, then returns south on paved roads from Manigotagan. Extend the Forests and Falls Tour (p.29) with these gravel roads.

Gravel Road Routes Summaries

A. Listed Alphabetically (as they appear in the book)

(The numbers preceding the route names represent their locations on the Summary Map.)

1. Lavenham Area / 85
2. Netley Marsh Ride / 87
3. Pembina Valley / 91
4. River Road Heritage Ride / 95

5. Roseisle and St. Lupicin / 99
6. South of Riding Mountain / 101
7. Treesbank Circuit / 105

B. Listed Geographically

Winnipeg-Selkirk:
Netley Marsh Ride
River Road Heritage Ride

Central and Southwestern:
Lavenham Area
Pembina Valley
Roseisle and St. Lupicin
Treesbank Circuit

Parklands:
South of Riding Mountain

C. Listed by Difficulty

(The symbol + denotes that the ride is also found in a harder category)

Easy:
Netley Marsh Ride +
River Road Heritage Ride
Treesbank Circuit +

Moderate:
Netley Marsh Ride
Pembina Valley (PR423) +
Roseisle and St. Lupicin
South of Riding Mountain
Treesbank Circuit

Difficult:
Lavenham Area
Pembina Valley (Mowbray)
Pembina Valley (PR423)
Pembina Valley (Snowflake)

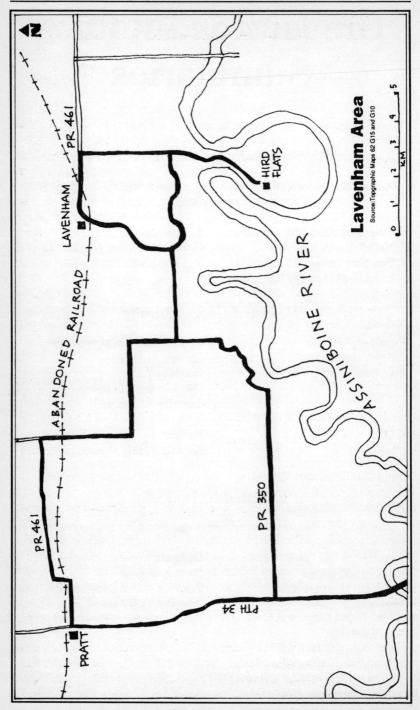

Lavenham Area

Source: Topographic Maps 62 G15 and G10

The Lavenham Area

Cycling PR 350 in southcentral Manitoba is both rewarding and demanding. The section from PTH 34 to the hamlet of Lavenham is a gem of a gravel road ride, with hills, scenery and little traffic. The rises of the Pembina Hills meet the folds of the Assiniboine River, combining into enough hills to dispel any myths about flat Manitoba. Cycle past aspens, bur oak and spruce, interspersed with the occasional homestead and stunning views of the river valley.

The road to Lavenham is best suited for fit cyclists looking for a hill ride. Enjoy out-and-back day rides; the return offers a different perspective of the hills and the views. Consider pre-arranged pick-ups, loops, or exploratory cruising throughout the area. Be cautious in your planning, as the hills and the sandy surface transform kilometers on a map into much longer distances on a bike. Frolicking along this road is fun at any time of the cycling season, but fall colors splash spectacularly across the valley. Choose the Lavenham Road after heavy rains have turned other routes to mud. One basic ride is described, with suggestions for further explorations of this hilly and beautiful slice of Manitoba, plus connections to other prime cycling areas in the region.

Type: Gravel road day rides.
Access: Access PR 350 and the Lavenham area from PTH 34. A good base for day rides is to park at the wayside park just north of the Assiniboine River on PTH 34. Alternately, drive to Lavenham from PR 242, and park there.
Facilities: None along PR 350 or in riding area. Nearest full facilities at Holland, at junction of PTHs 2 and 34. Camping at Spruce Woods Provincial Heritage Park.
Distance: PR 350 from PTH 34 to Lavenham is 20 km one way. Many shorter or longer rides possible.
Difficulty: Difficult (moderate to difficult distances; difficult hills and surface).

From the wayside park on PTH 34 beside the Assiniboine River, grunt up the hill on PTH 34 north and away from the river. Turn east (right) off the pavement onto the signposted PR 350. Skim along this initial section of gentle hills, past an unusual forest of tall, spreading spruces with clusters of young deciduous growth underneath. Soon the inclines get steeper, the poplars, ash and maples get taller, and there is an overall descent towards the snaking bends of the river.

Turn north (left) at the first T-junction. To the south is one of many dead end roads, leading to farmyards or fields in the river's floodplain. PR 350 now twists and turns to the northeast, following the general direction of the river. Watch for grand valley views. Near a brightly painted farm, the road swings north and uphill, leading to a sharp signposted turn to the east (right). Look behind you for a good view. Now the road really rollicks, zipping past fields fringed with forests, and great glimpses of the Assiniboine. At a steep and sandy junction of several roads, PR 350 climbs to the north (sharp left). The road now climbs north, east, then north again to Lavenham.

There are numerous options for returning to the wayside park, or for adding extra kilometers and hills. There is sufficient variety in the hills to make a return along the same route seem like a different road. A slight variation is to circle east and south of Lavenham, rejoining PR 350 at the steep and sandy junction. To ride this loop, cycle through Lavenham, turning east (right) onto PR 461. Ride 2.5 km on this road, passing one turn to the south and the abandoned rail line. Turn south (right) at the next municipal road, scooting past farmland and bush. Turn west (right) towards PR 350 at the first junction in this direction. Before taking that road, investigate the continuation of the road straight south, which apparently crosses a steep spit of land which widens and ends in Hird Flats (this has not been checked by bicycle). Follow the turnoff to PR 350 straight west as it screams in and out of a tributary valley. Several roads and trails branch off in this area, many with huge hills. Ask permission before crossing private land. At the steep and sandy junction the return route is due west (slightly to the left).

An alternate return is along PR 461 west from Lavenham. Twisting in virtually every compass direction, this route is far from the river and its hills, offering pleasant but not exciting riding. Use topographic maps 62 G/15 and 62 G/10 to plan your own investigation of the hummocky hills of the Lavenham area including the drop-off of the Manitoba Escarpment. The topographic maps show numerous trails in the area. Much of the land here is crown land, but is leased to farmers for forage crops: ask permission before crossing.

Exploring the Lavenham region is readily combined with other cycling adventures. Mountain bikers enjoying Spruce Woods (p.175) can extend their tire tracks westward. Add an extra day of gravel road exploring to the paved road pleasures of the Mouse and Turtle Tour (p.36). Use accommodation in Glenboro as a base for explorations throughout the region, including diversions into the Tiger Hills (p.81) and a westward extension of the Treesbank Circuit (p.105).

Netley Marsh Ride

The Netley Marshes herald the end of a long journey northward for the Red River, and serve as a destination for a much shorter cycling route. Twisting and turning with the river, PR 320 provides a delightful and easy day trip, or a short and pleasant overnight tour. It is an excellent family ride, with lots to see and do along the route and at the marsh. Enjoy the river scenery and delve into the history of this ribbon of Manitoba. Ride to Netley Creek at all times of the cycling season, but be prepared for heavier traffic when the fishing is good.

Type: Gravel road day rides and tours.
Access: The ride begins and ends on Main St. in Selkirk; longer rides could begin anywhere further south (e.g. Winnipeg or the River Road).
Facilities: Stores in Selkirk. Latrines and picnic tables at Breezy Point wayside park. Campsites, drinking water, latrines and snacks at Netley Creek Recreation Park.
Distance: 16 km one way from Selkirk, or 42 km one way from the Perimeter Highway in Winnipeg, following the River Road Heritage Parkway.
Difficulty: Easy to moderate (depending on distance; easy hills).

Before heading out on the ride to Netley Marsh along PR 320, stop at the Marine Museum in Selkirk to set the theme of the river and its human history. Cycle Main Street north out of the city. The road is initially paved, passing a seaplane base before going under the new bridge across the river. Catch glimpses of the river among the farms, homes, and lush groves of Manitoba maples, elms and poplars.

Further north, the road becomes gravel and the homes grade into cottages. Avoid the potholes and bounce over rough spots as you follow the constant turns. Breezy Point wayside park pops up around a bend: stop here for a rest and for a first glimpse of marsh vegetation as the river slows towards the delta.

Pedal a few kilometers further to reach the end of the road and the Netley Creek Recreation Park. Picnic or camp at the park, and investigate the exhibits of natural and human history. The Netley Marshes spawn large bird and fish populations before the water spreads into Lake Winnipeg. The historical significance of the junction of the Red River and Netley Creek relates to the first permanent encampment of the Saulteaux chief Pequis in 1795.

Return to Selkirk by the same riverside ride, or slip onto the bridge just north of the city and cross to the east bank to investigate historic St. Peter's Church.

Extensions to this route or possibilities for connections to other routes abound. For a longer day ride or tour, start further south along the Red River.

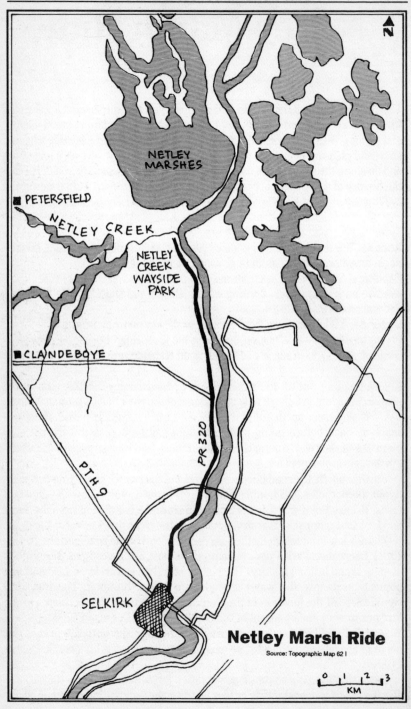

NETLEY MARSHES

■ PETERSFIELD

NETLEY CREEK

NETLEY CREEK WAYSIDE PARK

■ CLANDEBOYE

PR 320

PTH 9

SELKIRK

Netley Marsh Ride

Source: Topographic Map 62 I

0 1 2 3
KM

From Winnipeg, ride a historic route along the River Road Heritage Parkway (p.95), dropping in at Fort Garry (p.33) on the way to Selkirk. Consider an alternate return along the east bank of the river, although these roads are largely paved (p.26). Towards the northern end connect PR 320 with The Road to Hecla (p.58), which heads north to the beaches of Lake Winnipeg.

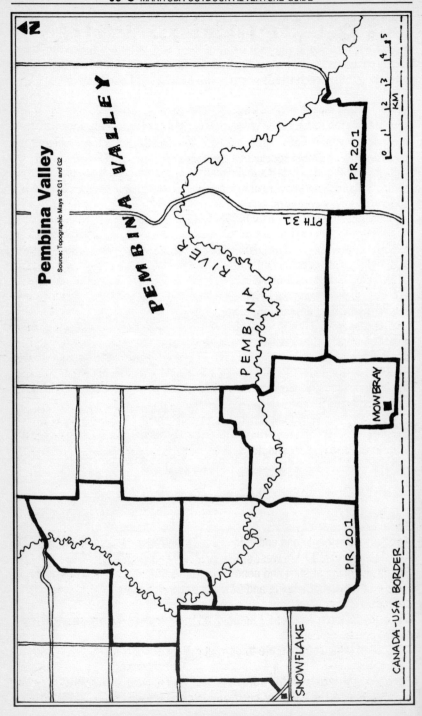

Pembina Valley

Source: Topographic Mays 62 G1 and G2

PEMBINA VALLEY

PEMBINA RIVER

PTH 31

PR 201

PR 201

MOWBRAY

SNOWFLAKE

CANADA–USA BORDER

N

KM
0 1 2 3 4 5

The Pembina Valley

The Pembina River snakes across the plateau of the Manitoba Escarpment in southcentral Manitoba. The present day trickle belies the force of the glacial meltwaters which cut a wide but steep valley through the shales of the escarpment. The most spectacular scenery lies south of La Riviere, where the valley width is compressed and the walls rise sheer or in tight tiers. While the rolling uplands sport covers of wheat and canola, thick forests of ash and oak soften the valley contours.

This is back road heaven for hill-addicted mountain bikers. The vertical rise is among the steepest found on Manitoba gravel roads, and it recurs with exhausting frequency. The scenery is spectacular, the descents are exhilarating, and the ride goes on and on for kilometers. These qualities and the lack of facilities in the area limit riding possibilities for less serious or less athletic cyclists. Short out-and-back rides are possible, but to see the best of the valley requires traveling demanding distances.

There are two day-trip loops that show off the best of the valley's scenery and topography: the first starts from Mowbray on the U.S.A. border, and the second begins south of La Riviere, where PR 423 crosses the Pembina River. An extended one-way ride requiring pick-up or a car shuttle stretches between the bridge on PR 201 (northeast of Windygates) and Snowflake. Shorter out-and-back day rides can be started from virtually any point in the Valley.

Regardless of how far and where you ride, come to this region prepared. Carry more water and food than you think you'll need, and repair equipment. Longer distance riders should carry topographic maps 62 G/1 and 62 G/2.

Mowbray Loop

Type: Gravel road day rides.
Access: Rides begin and end in Mowbray, located on PR 201 along the American border, 11 km west of the southern end of PTH 31.
Facilities: None at start and none along route. Nearest full facilities in La Riviere or Morden; camping and B&B accommodation on PR 423 where it crosses the river.
Distance: Shorter loop of 27 km, and a longer loop of 47 km; shorter routes can be ridden.
Difficulty: Difficult (moderate to difficult distances; difficult hills).

From the ghost town of Mowbray ride due east for 3 km along PR 201. Swing north (left) with the highway, but do not follow it when it turns east 1.6 km later.

Continue north to the first descent, at a point where the valley wall is broken into a broad tier. The second stage of the descent carries you down with a turn to the valley floor proper. Cross the Pembina River and the first climb looms ahead for 2 heart-pounding km. Turn west (left) at the top, then just 1.6 km later shift south (left). Follow the trees and the curves in an initially steep then gradual descent back to the valley bottom, and a T-junction. At this point you have ridden 17 km and climbed or descended a total of 320 m.

For the shortest return, turn south (left), crossing the river then climbing out of the broad bend of the valley. The final leg of the climb is tough, with the recent straightening of the road adding a few more meters of vertical. For the rest of the ride the flat plateau prevails. Follow the road south to the junction with PR 201. Turn east (left), following the road as it jogs south back to Mowbray.

For those wanting more kilometers and greater training effect, turn north (right) at the T-junction in the river valley. Climb back up the valley with a short but steep climb. Cruise easily along the agricultural plain before taking the first gravel road to the west (left). It's an exhilarating descent into one of the loveliest parts of the Pembina Valley. There are pastures and wheat fields with solitary ashes in the valley, with the contours fringed by oak and aspen. Follow the turns of the road, crossing the river one last time. At the next T-junction, turn south (left), and puff up to the plateau. After 2 km this road is joined by PR 201. Continue south on the final 12 km along the turns of PR 201 back to Mowbray, with only a shallow dip across Snowflake Creek for topographic relief.

PR 423 Loop

Type: Gravel road day rides.
Access: This circle ride begins and ends on PR 423, where it crosses the Pembina River. Reach this point from La Riviere by driving south on PR 242 for 10 km, then turning east (left) onto PR 423, following it to the bridge. Park off the road.
Facilities: Camping and B&B accommodation on PR 423 at the start. No other facilities along route. Nearest full facilities in La Riviere or Morden.
Distance: Full circle ride is 31 km. Shorter out-and-back trips possible.
Difficulty: Difficult (moderate distance; difficult hills).

Enjoy this shorter and less arduous, but equally scenic route. Ride clockwise, following PR 423 to the east as it climbs steeply out of the valley; look back and admire the view. Don't follow the provincial road at the crest, but instead turn south (right) at the T-junction. The road rolls up and down the upper contours of the valley before taking a series of 90 degree turns to avoid a tributary's trench. Take the first gravel road to the west (right) and gracefully swoop into the pastoral pleasures of the valley. Follow the sharp turns of the road, cross the river, then turn north (right) at the T-junction. This is approximately the half-way point, at 17 km from the start.

After traveling north for 1.6 km, the road veers west (left) and confronts the steepest climb of the ride. Grunt, pedal and push up, then take the first road to the north (right), for a relaxing 3 km on level ground. Grab the first road to the east (right), and scream down the valley wall, braking hard to make the sharp turn to the north (left). It's up again for 75 m over the next 3 km, ending in a T-junction. Turn east (right) and sail back into the valley to the starting point.

PR 201 to Snowflake

Type: Gravel road day rides.
Access: This is a one way ride, requiring pre-arranged pick-up or a car shuttle. The start is on PR 201, on the bridge across the Pembina River. There is a parking area next to the bridge. Reach it approximately 30 km along PR 432 and PR 201 from Morden. The ride ends in Snowflake, 21 km south of La Riviere on PR 242.
Facilities: None at start and end, and none along route. Nearest full facilities in La Riviere or Morden; camping and B&B accommodation on PR 423 where it crosses the river.
Distance: One way of 49 km.
Difficulty: Difficult (distance and hills).

With over 500 m of grudging ascent or flying descent packed into 49 km of gravel road, this is a tough but rewarding ride. The ride starts on PR 201, where the Pembina River valley is the narrowest, and thick forests coat the steep walls. Several kilometers of easy, level spinning are also included, but the route swoops in and out of the Pembina Valley up to five times.

From the bridge, climb with PR 201 up to the top of the plateau. Follow the turn of this road to the west (right), and continue straight to PTH 31. Turn north (right) onto the paved highway for 1.6 km; turn west (left) onto a gravel road, which partly descends the valley to a T-junction. This route now merges with Route A. Turn north (right), following the road down and around to the river, then climb up the opposite valley wall. Turn west (left) at the first gravel road, travel for 1.6 km before turning south (left) and descending into the valley. At the T-junction turn north (right; 28 km from the start) and climb steeply up. Take the first gravel road to the west (left) and swing with it down and around to another T-junction. Turn north (right) and follow it to the steepest climb of the ride. Once on the plateau take the second road to the south (left), and continue on it to the hamlet of Snowflake.

There are even more hills in the Pembina Valley waiting to be explored. Virtually all the land in the valley is privately owned; ask permission before exploring inviting trails. Meet the challenges of the Pembina Valley in conjunction with several paved road rides. PTH 31 (p.51) cuts through the valley on its way to Windygates. Extend the Rock Lake Tour (p.62) with a day or two of adventuring in the southern valley.

River Road Heritage Ride

Cycling the River Road Heritage Parkway is an excursion into the history of the Red River and the Winnipeg area. Over seven historical points of interest, many with exhibits, are sprinkled along this scenic, winding road. This is an ideal route for family excursions with its short distances, gentle hills, and interesting scenery.

The Parkway is gravel but heavily oiled, keeping it accessible under all weather conditions. Traffic can be high on weekends, but the speed limit is low. Ride the River Road Heritage Parkway as a day trip, or follow the suggestions for extending the route.

Type: Gravel road day rides.
Access: Eight km north of Winnipeg's Perimeter Highway, the River Road Heritage Parkway (PR 238) leads off PTH 9. Northern access from PTH 44. Cycle or drive to either access. Parking at several wayside picnic areas.
Facilities: Latrines and picnic facilities at wayside parks, and at some historic locations. Snacks or meals at Kennedy House on the Parkway, or at Lockport.
Distance: One way along the Parkway is 12 km. Return loop from the Perimeter Highway of Winnipeg is 40 km. Longer rides possible.
Difficulty: Easy (distance and hills).

The beginning of the River Road Heritage Parkway (PR 238) is marked by a stone monument. The Parkway initially travels east, then runs north parallel to the Red River. At this turn, a plaque at the wayside park introduces the area's history. History is replaced by sumptuous new homes until Scotts House is reached, a small building left open to the elements to illustrate construction methods. Twin Oaks demurely awaits your next stop. Constructed in 1850, this solid stone structure served as a girls' school, and is now a private residence.

The road now swings up against a sweeping turn of the river, where riprap restrains erosion of the bank. The spires of St. Andrew's Church encourage you around the curve and up the hill. St. Andrew's is the oldest stone church in western Canada, constructed in 1849. Together with the St. Andrew's National Historic Park, it depicts the early history of white agricultural settlement of the Red River, and in particular, the role of religion and missionaries.

The smell of fresh baked scones lures you on to Kennedy House. Built of

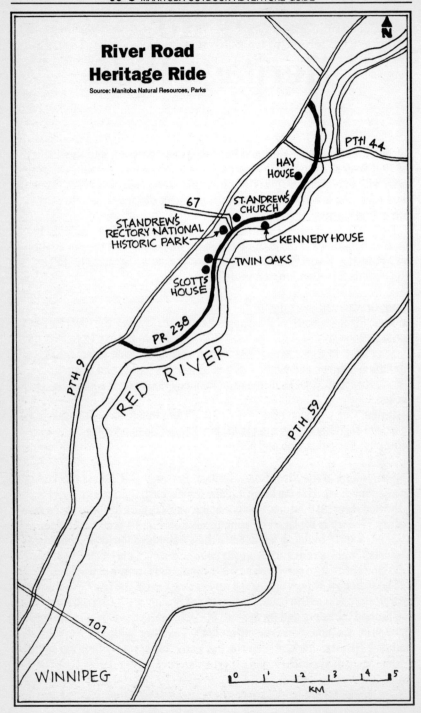

River Road Heritage Ride

Source: Manitoba Natural Resources, Parks

N

HAY HOUSE

PTH 44

ST. ANDREW'S CHURCH

67

ST. ANDREW'S RECTORY NATIONAL HISTORIC PARK

KENNEDY HOUSE

TWIN OAKS

SCOTT'S HOUSE

PR 238

PTH 9

RED RIVER

PTH 59

707

WINNIPEG

0   1   2   3   4   5
KM

stone in 1866 for Capt. William Kennedy, a Hudson Bay Co. trader, arctic explorer and lay missionary, it houses both a tea room and a museum. Take a break, eat, and relax in the beautiful garden bordering the Red River. Another stone house and display marks the northern end of the Red River Heritage Parkway.

The Heritage Parkway ends at St. Andrew's Locks with a further display about settlement of the Red River. The easiest return journeys are either back along River Road or via the paved PTH 9 (note that this is a high traffic route) There are several possibilities to extend the ride. North of PTH 44, River Road quickly leads to Lower Fort Garry National Historic Park. Connect with Henderson Highway (PR 204) to return along the east bank of the Red (see the Lockport Loop p.33), or make the River Road Heritage Parkway part of the Birds Hill Bop (p.25) or the Netley Creek ride (p.87).

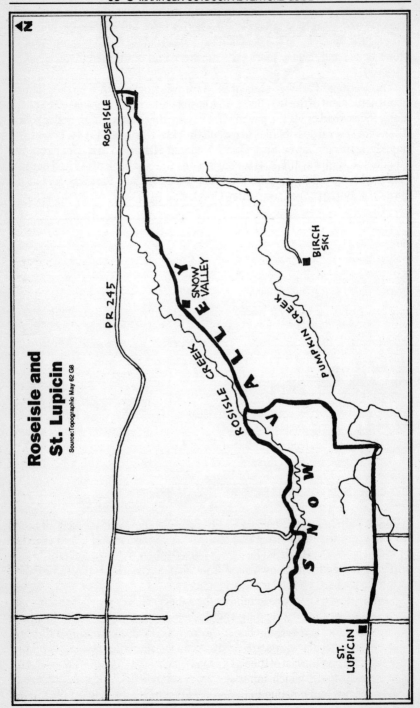

Roseisle and St. Lupicin

Source:Topographic May 62 G8

Roseisle and St. Lupicin

The Roseisle-St. Lupicin area provides boundless gravel road cycling through a landscape which is both attractive and challenging. Known as Snow Valley, this area is tucked into the edge of the Pembina Hills, where the 150 m rise over 10 km identifies the Manitoba Escarpment. Hills fold steeply around creeks and streams, and thick aspen and oak forests hug the valley walls.

A network of gravel and back roads provides hours of cycling pleasure, for all ages and abilities. The 'classic' loop through the area is described in detail below, and several additional routes are suggested. Develop a little familiarity with the area, then just explore: good scenery and challenging riding is guaranteed. Fall is an especially beautiful time in Snow Valley. The gravel roads dry quickly after rain, but heavy mud faces cyclists on some of the municipal and farm roads after rain and in the spring. The off road cycling is also superb in the Snow Valley area (p.171).

Type: Gravel road day rides.
Access: The best access is via Roseisle, located 26 km west of Carman, and just off PR 245. Park in Roseisle, or follow the directions below and park off the road within Snow Valley.
Facilities: Store in Roseisle. Camping in Stephenfield Provincial Recreation Park. Restaurant in Notre Dame de Lourdes. Nearest full facilities in Carman.
Distance: Loop between Roseisle and St. Lupicin is 25 km. Other distances possible.
Difficulty: Moderate (distances; moderate to difficult hills).

A 25 km loop between Roseisle and St. Lupicin shows off the best of Snow Valley. From the main street of Roseisle cruise west past the first junction (which leads to the Birch Ski Resort). After a few bends the road climbs briefly and then descends into Snow Valley. Immediately to the left is the Snow Valley Ski Resort, where off road trails originate.

For the next 6 km the road follows the valley, at times paralleling Roseisle Creek, at other times ascending and descending the valley walls. Continue straight past the next two junctions (the first one is where the loop ultimately returns). Spectacular views are the rewards for climbing the next two hills. After descending the last of these, the road reaches a T-junction; take the road to the south (left), which immediately crosses Roseisle Creek. The road climbs steadily, culminating in the last steep uphill of the ride. At the top the road turns south to the hamlet of St. Lupicin, distinguished by its craft gallery for local artisans.

Leave St. Lupicin by the gravel road to the east (to your right when facing the gallery), and follow its bends and dips, ignoring any turnoffs. It soon degenerates into a farm road. After descending back into Snow Valley, turn east (right) and follow the now familiar road back to Roseisle.

There are numerous other possibilities for exploring the network of gravel roads in the area. For example, take the road past the Birch Ski area and follow it and other roads up the escarpment further south. Inspect the various roads leading off the main loop, including a turn to the north (right) at the T-junction. Use topographical maps 62 G/8 and 62 G/9 for further inspiration.

South of Riding Mountain

A vast network of gravel provincial and municipal roads slips through the rolling parkland south of Riding Mountain National Park. Hills, trees and lakes sculpt wonderful gravel road pedaling, with enough distance and variety to suit all levels of cyclists. The region merits exploration in its own right, but it also combines with the back roads and trails of Riding Mountain National Park for superb long distance touring (p.154). Sidetrack from the paved road Riding Mountain Tour (p.54) for a day or more of gravel road discovery. Ride up the face of the Manitoba Escarpment, scoot up and down stream valleys, and traverse the vast Birdtail River Valley.

This area is best suited to fit cyclists hungry for hills, and with a sense of exploration and direction. It is ideal for mountain bikers wanting varied and exciting day rides from a fixed base. Campgrounds, farm vacation, B&B, and hotel accommodation facilitate exploration of the nooks and crannies of the area. Make tire tracks at any time of the cycling season. The gravel roads remain in good condition, although some of the municipal roads become slick after heavy rain.

Read the general descriptions below, grab a map, and pedal. Wander these gravel roads and discover your own favorite route. The greatest difficulty is navigation, as the roads crisscross in a confusing maze. Bring the provincial highway map, as the Provincial Roads are clearly marked, and are signposted at junctions. These roads are a good introduction to the area. To decipher the myriad municipal roads, use topographic maps or municipal road maps. Unfortunately, the most useful scale of topographic maps (the 1:250,000 scale of 62 J and 62 K) are 25 years out of date, at the time of writing. Most of the roads are still shown accurately, although the status of some, especially gravel versus paved, may have changed. Municipal road maps are accurate, although 10 years out of date, but several are needed. Maps for the Rural Municipalities of Clan William, Rosedale, and Rossburn, and the Local Government District of Park, cover most of the area.

Type: Gravel road day rides and tours.
Access: Unlimited access. This area stretches for over 100 km south of Riding Mountain, and is bounded or intersected by PTHs 5, 10 and 45 and several Provincial Roads.
Facilities: Few facilities along the gravel roads, apart from scattered farm

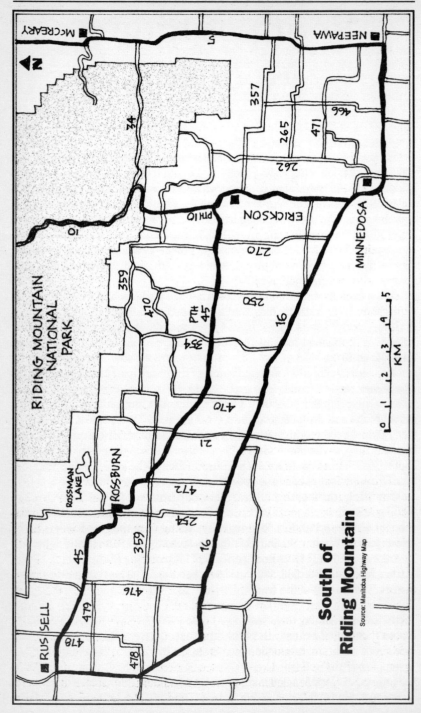

South of Riding Mountain

Source: Manitoba Highway Map

vacations or B&B. Camping at several campgrounds in area, or inside Riding Mountain National Park. Full or partial facilities in many of the towns along the bounding highways, including Neepawa, Minnedosa, Erickson, Rossburn, and Russell.

Distance: Unlimited choice.

Difficulty: Moderate (easy to difficult distances; moderate to difficult hills).

The area south of Riding Mountain can be broken roughly into three blocks: eastern, central and western. The eastern block is the smallest, lying between PTHs 5 and 10, and is dominated by the rise of the Manitoba Escarpment. PRs 265 and 471 are challenging and scenic rides, with long climbs up the escarpment in several stages. Streams cut further creases into this landscape of fields, pastures and forests. Several circuits are possible, especially in combination with some of the paved roads, such as PR 357 (part of the paved road Riding Mountain Tour p.54).

North of PR 357, PRs 262 and 263 mimic the park boundaries, heading east from Onanole, then swinging south, east, and finally north to the park boundary and a connection with the Rolling River Road and ultimately PR 19. Very fit cyclists could consider riding this as a full loop of 68 km from Wasagaming in a demanding day. Alternatively, take a two day tour from Erickson, camping overnight at Whirlpool Lake (7 km extra return). Cycle on PR 357 and its connection with PR 262 both going and returning, to avoid lengthy stints on PTH 10.

The central block lies west of Erickson and PTH 10, and stretches towards Rossman Lake. Pick and choose among the many municipal roads which lace this hummocky land, splashed with hundreds of lakes and sloughs. Tall aspens alternate with pasture and the occasional field. PR 359 is a pleasantly hilly gravel road entrance into Lake Audy. The turnoff is not officially signposted. An advertisement for the Lake Audy Store may indicate the junction, but rely on map navigation to identify the turn. Cyclists are not allowed to cross the bison enclosure because of vulnerability to the large animals.

The back roads of this central block supplement off road tours through Riding Mountain National Park. Connect the Long Lake Road and the Grasshopper Valley (p.160) in a 55 km tour by cycling from the gated access to the Heron Creek Warden Station, east and north along PR 359, to the turnoff north to Lake Audy. Baldy Lake Road and Long Lake could also be connected south of the park along PRs 566, 577 and 359 (p.161; tour of 95 km). Quick directions are as follows: ride south from the Baldy Lake Warden Station past the park boundary; turn west (right) at T-junction for 0.5 km; turn south (left) and ride to the cairn at Marco; turn east (right) onto PR 577; follow the turn of PR 577 south (right) to junction with PR 566; turn east (left) and follow the turn of PR 566 south (right) to the junction with PR 359; turn east (left) and follow it to the gated turnoff to the Heron Creek Warden Station, which is 1.6 km after PR 359 turns north. Check detailed maps for short cuts along municipal roads. Several campsites can be selected within the park, and a slight detour west at Marco along PR 577 to Rossman Lake provides camping at the southern leg of the circuit. For both of these routes, remember to register in advance for free camping at the primitive campsites along the Central Road in the park, and also check on the current conditions of the Long Lake Road.

The third and western block lies west of Rossman Lake and encompasses the magnificent Birdtail Valley. PR 254 cuts straight north through the valley, with a terrifying, curving descent (or agonizing ascent) into the wide valley cut by glacial meltwaters. PR 254 leads into the Deep Lake Warden Station and Campground, and to the western end of the Central Road (p.158). The entrance to the park is not marked: at the second jog to the west of PR 254, keep going north on a narrow and unassuming road.

A three day circle tour starting from Rossman Lake could link Baldy Lake Road and the Central Road of Riding Mountain National Park (p.158; total tour of 90 km). Ride east from Rossman Lake on PR 577, turning north (left) at Marco to reach the Baldy Lake Trail (via a short jog east (right) then north (left) again). Tour Baldy Lake Road and the western end of the Central Road, with overnight stops at Gunn Creek campsite and the Deep Lake Campground. Cycle south from Deep Lake along PR 254, turning east (left) onto a paved section of PR 577 to return to Rossman Lake. The western extension of PR 254 also merits a ride, as it rapidly rolls through avenues of poplars. Set out and discover the many other delightful rides on the gravel roads south of Riding Mountain National Park.

The Treesbank Circuit

The Treesbank Circuit is a delightful two day tour in central Manitoba, showcasing hill, prairie and river environments. The tour runs south and east from Brandon, zipping over the Brandon Hills and cruising across farmland to the Assiniboine River. Slip across the river on one of Manitoba's last ferries. The return route traces a historic period in Manitoba's exploration, as the roads skirts close to the ruins of several fur trading forts.

This is a tour in transition, with changes in road surface, bridge construction and ferry location altering the route in the future, hopefully increasing the gravel road touring possibilities. The present route is described, plus a possible future scenario. Several variations on the basic route are possible, providing alternatives to hilly or straight road sections, and there are several ways to extend the tour. Cycle day rides out-and-back along the route, or find loops among the municipal roads in all cycling seasons. The roads may become muddy in places after rain, and the route is too exposed for comfortable cool weather riding. The tour is enjoyable with only a little cycling experience.

Type: Gravel road day rides and tours.
Access: The tour begins from the southeastern end of Brandon. Two routes are possible: either cycle due south on 17th Street, or follow PR 344 east then south from Richmond Ave. The tour returns on the north bank of the Assiniboine River, via PR 457, with an alternate return to the southeastern corner of the city.
Facilities: Full facilities in Brandon, Wawanesa and Glenboro, with very limited facilities in between. No public access to facilities on Canadian Forces Base Shilo.
Distance: Basic loop via the Brandon Hills and return via Shilo is 90 km. Alternate routes longer.
Difficulty: Moderate (moderate distances; easy to moderate hills).

The present two day tour heads for overnight accommodation in Wawanesa. From Brandon, select one of the two starts to the Treesbank Circuit. The extension of 17th Street leads due south to the ridge of the Brandon Hills, and offers a challenging climb and delightful descent, the only real hills of the ride. Midway on the hill, you'll pass the entrance to wonderful off road skimming in the Brandon Hills Wildlife Management Area (p.127). Flash past aspen and bur oak on the descent to a T-junction with PR 453. Turn east (left), and follow the turns of the road, descending to the junction with PR 344. Turn south (right) onto PR 344.

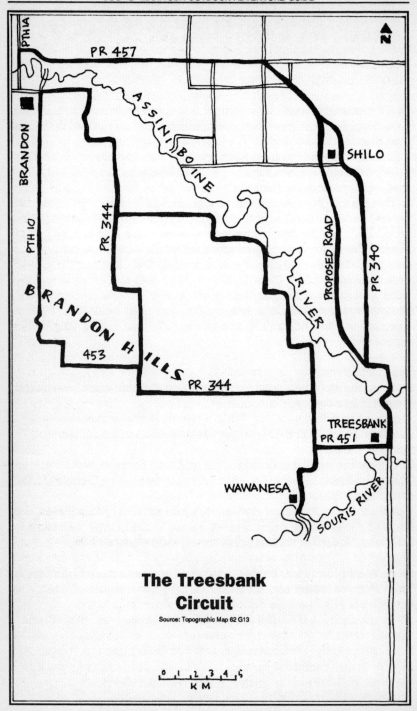

The Treesbank
Circuit

Source: Topographic Map 62 G13

If you'd rather avoid the hills and trees of this route, select PR 344 in Brandon and cruise south through farmland, passing east of the abrupt and 'bald' edge of the Brandon Hills. Continue past the junction with PR 453.

Level terrain characterizes the rest of the day's ride, but there are almost constant vistas of hills to the west and to the south. Continue on PR 344, turning east towards the river, then spinning easily south, noting the junction with PR 451. To reach Wawanesa (33 km; full facilities), continue on PR 344, dipping in and out of Black Creek, and finally screaming down the banks of the Souris River into town.

There are two choices for the return trip: across the river past Shilo, or a winding back road exploration on the west bank of the river. To follow the first route, retrace your tire tracks to the junction with PR 451. Turn east (right) and zip through Treesbank, veering north (left) at the junction with PR 340. Cruise past aspen and pasture to a rustic descent to the low riverbanks and the ferry. The directions on the other side are easy: follow the newly relocated PR 340 around the initial jog north then west, then ride straight north, past pasture and irrigated fields, to the west of Shilo. At the junction with PR 457, turn west (left) to return to Brandon.

The alternate return maximizes riverbank views but requires topographic maps 62 G/12 and 62 G/13. Start by cycling north from Wawanesa on PR 344, cycling past the junction with PR 451. Instead of following PR 344 as it swings west, continue straight north. Use the topographic maps to cycle this basic pattern: north until stopped by the river, then west (left) to the next road north (usually 1.6 km apart; right turn). Continue in this pattern to the eastern extremity of Brandon, or cycle due west on any municipal route to reconnect with PR 344 and a more direct route back to the city.

Add extra kilometers to the tour by staying a second night in Wawanesa. Spend a day exploring the south bank of the Assiniboine River towards Stockton and Glenboro (full facilities). Use topographic maps 62 G/11 and 62 G/12 as your guide. Long distance riders can connect the Treesbank Circuit with the off road delights of Spruce Woods Provincial Heritage Park (p.175), or the hills of the Lavenham area (p.85).

A bridge will replace the Treesbank Ferry for the 1990 cycling season, and PR 340 may be paved within 5 years. Future tourers could still return to Brandon on PR 340, or the alternative gravel road route west of the river could be followed. The ferry is rumored to be destined for downstream Stockton, opening up further gravel and back road explorations on the north and south banks of the river, including the Assiniboine Corridor Wildlife Management Area. Check with Manitoba Highways on the status of the ferry.

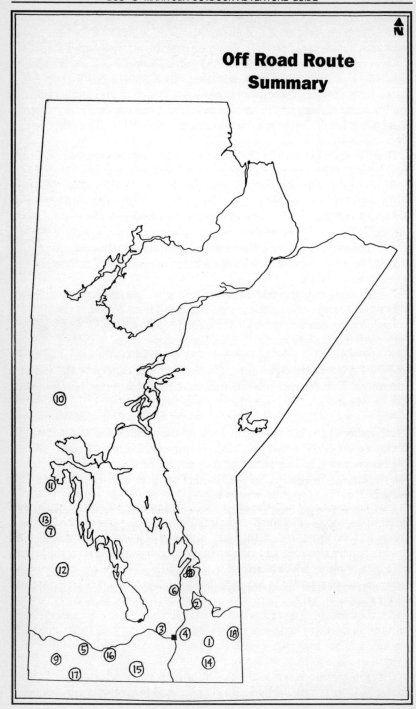

Off Road Route Summary

OFF ROAD RIDING

Mountain bikes have started a new revolution in Manitoban cycling. These fat-tired bikes with wide handlebars were designed by cyclists determined to ride away from paved and gravel roads. The concept has caught on, with mountain bikes sales growing with the evolution of the design and components. Many Manitobans use the bikes to survive potholes in the city, extend their cycling season into the winter, or toot around cottage back roads. In addition, mountain bikes are introducing Manitobans and visitors to corners of the province which they didn't previously know, and they are adding a new dimension to familiar ground. It's an exciting sport which is transporting Manitobans out of the cities and towns and into the backcountry and wilderness.

Nineteen different off road routes have been selected, spanning all levels of difficulty and all parts of the province. 'Off road' in this book refers to cycling which is not on provincial highways and roads, nor on gravel municipal roads. Most of the routes are in provincial parks and forests. Over half of the routes follow easy spinning roads which offer low rolling resistance and require no technical skills (although some are challenging in their length and their hills). Often too long or open to appeal to hikers, the roads are ideal for cyclists. Other routes twist and turn along cross country ski and snowmobile trails. Cycling difficulty ranges from the gentle, easy trails of Birds Hill Provincial Park, to the technically tough Biathlon Ski Trail at Falcon Lake in the Whiteshell.

Designated hiking and equestrian trails have been excluded, with four exceptions: Birds Hill, Hecla Island, Spruce Woods, and Turtle Mountain. Cycling is compatible with the other trail uses in these cases because of trail width, topography or location. Although Parks Branch has granted permission to include these trails in the book, always check with Parks staff for trail conditions and closures, and yield to hikers and horses. Many of the hiking trails in provincial parks which are not described in this book are too short, too technical, or too crowded to accommodate mountain bikes. Please respect trail designations.

A few trails described in this book are located on private land: please check with the landowners indicated, and treat their property well. Remember that you ride at your own risk. Please respect the property rights of other land owners and ask permission before crossing their land.

Off road touring is not as developed as its paved road cousin, except in Riding Mountain National Park. Touring is possible in other areas, but more ingenuity is required since campsites or accommodation are infrequent. The possibilities for mountain bike touring increase considerably when gravel roads (p.81) are thrown in. The key constraint to your imagination is accommodation: check the provincial accommodation guide carefully, remembering that vacation farms and B&B are often tucked away in remote corners of Manitoba.

To find an off road route suited to your interests and abilities, review the overview map (p.108) and the summary table (p.112), then read the route descriptions . The route descriptions are structured similarly to the Paved Road and Gravel Road sections (see p.7, 'How to Use this Book'). Here, the 'Type' paragraph identifies day rides and tours, and indicates whether the route follows back roads or trails. Where possible, the 'Distance' paragraph lists kilometers for individual trails, otherwise a general indication of distances is provided.

Each of the 19 route descriptions includes detailed instructions for riding back roads or trails, plus suggestions for further exploring. The level of detail reflects the nature of the trail system: a straight road with no turnoffs requires less explanation than an interlocking set of short trails. In only a few cases, the complexity of an unsigned trail system defies written explanation: check the map and explore on your own. All the trails included here have been ridden thoroughly or partially. If a suggestion for additional riding has not been checked by bicycle, this is clearly stated. The information included in the route descriptions is as accurate as possible, but may change with time. Beavers, fallen trees and forest fires are key forces in altering trails. Trail improvements or re-routings may be planned by provincial and federal parks staff.

Unless indicated, additional maps besides the ones included here are unnecessary. For some of the more remote routes, topographic maps may be helpful and the numbers are supplied. Note that these maps often provide only general topographical features, e.g. identifying rivers or hills. In many cases the routes described are not on the topographic maps, which are often many years out of date. Routes drawn on the topographic maps may no longer exist. Air photos are the best source of current information.

The off road routes described in this book are intended to provide a comprehensive listing of the major rides in Manitoba. There are many other trails awaiting exploration. Build your confidence on the well-known routes, then expand your off road horizons with some original exploration.

Regardless of whether you are pushing back mountain biking frontiers in the Roaring River Canyon or skimming briefly at Birds Hill Provincial Park, be prepared when you ride. Always carry water, food, a map (e.g. the maps in this book) and tools. Inevitably you will need one or all of these. Contrary to common belief, mountain bikes do get flats, usually at the farthest point from the car. The other most common problem is a broken derailleur, especially when trail riding. Read up on repairs, fit a saddle bag to your bike, and fill it. The one time you don't is the one time you'll really need to.

Enjoy the trails from spring through fall. Select sandier routes in the spring or after rain, skipping them in a dry, hot summer. Listen to the radio or check with Department of Natural Resources for route closures from forest fire hazards. Fall mountain biking offers special delights when the leaves change colors and the bugs disappear. If it's a late fall, be careful of riding in provincial parks and forests after mid-November when deer hunting season starts. If you must, ride on Sundays when hunting is illegal, and wear bright clothing.

The final word: ride responsibly, respecting property and other trail users, but most of all explore and enjoy.

Off Road Routes Summaries

A. Listed Alphabetically (as they appear in the book)

(The numbers preceding the route names represent their locations on the Summary Map.)

B. Listed Geographically

General:
Off Road in Towns and Cities

Winnipeg and Selkirk:
Beaudry Prov. Heritage Park: North
Birds Hill Provincial Park

Eastern:
Agassiz Provincial Forest
The Beaches and Belair Provincial Forest
Sandilands Provincial Forest
Whiteshell Provincial Park

Central and Southwestern :
Brandon Hills
Lauder Sandhills Wildlife Management Area
Snow Valley and Birch
Spruce Woods Provincial Heritage Park
Turtle Mountain Provincial Park

Interlake:
Camp Morton Provincial Recreation Park
Hecla Island Back Roads

Parklands:
Duck Mountain Provincial Park and
    Forest
Porcupine Provincial Forest
Riding Mountain National Park
Roaring River Canyon

North:
Northern Off Road

C. Listed by Difficulty

(The symbol + denotes that the ride is also found in a harder category)

Easy:
Agassiz Provincial Forest +
The Beaches +
Beaudry Provincial Heritage Park
Birds Hill Provincial Park +
Brandon Hills +
Camp Morton
Hecla (west quarry)
Hecla (eastern shore) +
Lauder Sandhills WMA +
Off Road in Towns and Cities +
Riding Mountain National Park
    (several) +
Sandilands Provincial Forest (ski) +
Sandilands Provincial Forest
    (Whitemouth)
Sandilands Provincial Forest
    (roads) +
Spruce Woods (south) +
Turtle Mountain (east) +
Whiteshell (north) +
Whiteshell (central) +
Whiteshell (south) +

Moderate:
Agassiz Provincial Forest
The Beaches
Birds Hill Provincial Park
Brandon Hills
Duck Mountain (Route N) +
Hecla (eastern shore)
Lauder Sandhills WMA
Northern Off Road
Off Road in Towns and Cities

Moderate (continued)
Riding Mountain National Park
    (several) +
Sandilands Provincial Forest (ski)
Sandilands Provincial Forest
    (roads) +
Spruce Woods (south)
Spruce Woods (north) +
Turtle Mountain (west)
Turtle Mountain (east)
Whiteshell (north)
Whiteshell (central)
Whiteshell (south) +

Difficult:
Duck Mountain (Route N)
Duck Mountain (others)
Porcupine Provincial Forest (Bell
    site)
Porcupine Provincial Forest
    (Steeprock)
Riding Mountain (several)
Roaring River Canyon
Sandilands Provincial Forest
    (roads)
Snow Valley and Birch
Spruce Woods (north)
Whiteshell (south)

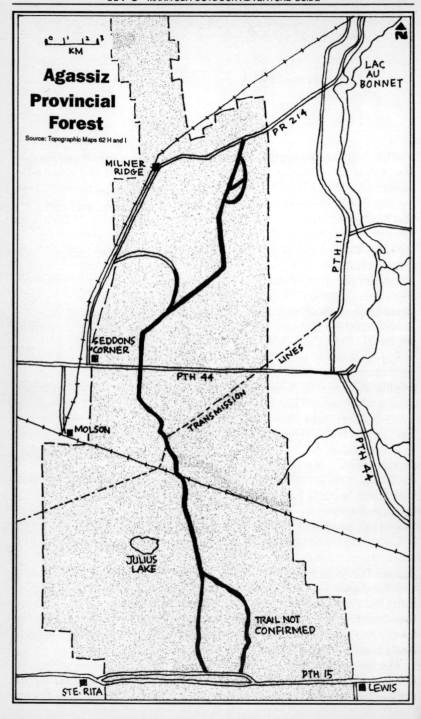

Agassiz Provincial Forest

Source: Topographic Maps 62 H and I

Agassiz Provincial Forest

Among the provincial forests forming a green line across southeastern Manitoba, Agassiz boasts the best back road riding. Although it lacks the beaches of Belair (p.117) and the trail and road network of Sandilands (p.166), the back roads in Agassiz offer delightful and fast spinning. Best of all, there is little sand for tires and spirits to sink into. The forest's proximity to Winnipeg and the gentle hills make it an excellent candidate for families or for cyclists building confidence with out-of-town riding. More advanced riders can enjoy fast-paced spinning away from traffic. Cycle the roads of Agassiz as a diversion during the paved road Forest and Falls Tour (p.29). The riding remains good here even with wet weather and during spring, but the open road is too exposed for comfortable cool weather cruising. The main disappointment is the lack of circle routes: most rides must be out-and-back, or pick-ups must be arranged.

Type: Off road day rides; back roads and trails.
Access: Agassiz Provincial Forest in southeastern Manitoba straddles PR 214 and PTHs 44 and 15. Trails are accessible from all of these. Key access points are: 6 km west of the junction with PTH 11 on PR 214 (trail to the south); 3 km east of Seddons Corner on PTH 44 (trails north and south); and 9 km east of Ste. Rita on PTH 15 (trails run north and south). No designated parking areas.
Facilities: None at trailheads or along trails. Spring water along PR 214 near PTH 11 (signposted). Stores and restaurants along access highways (e.g. Seddons Corner).
Distance: Varied, with over 50 km possible. No set trails.
Difficulty: Easy to moderate (depending on distance; easy hills).

A good quality gravel road runs the length of Agassiz Provincial Forest. Beginning from PR 214 in the north, it cuts diagonally to the southeast. This is the main riding artery, with trails diverging into the jack pine and aspen to the east and west. Cycling the curves and dips of the main road from any of the access points provides hours of cruising and exploration. There is a gradual north to south decline along the road.

The best opportunity for circle rides is at the northern end of Agassiz Provincial Forest, from the PR 214 access. For the first 5 km south along the central gravel road, a series of side trails loop off into the jack pines to the east (left). Soft pine needles form a solid but smooth riding surface across the rolling landscape. All the loops tested return to the central road.

The central road stretches between PR 214 and PTH 44 for 17 km. Less than 1 km north from PTH 44, a trail to the west (left) provides a brief but pleasant loop to a gravel pit and back to PTH 44; return to the starting point along the service road. From PTH 44 the road runs due north, then shifts to the northeast. Approximately 4 km from the parking area, a trail heads straight north, leading to a beaver pond.

Between PTHs 44 and 15 stretch 22 km of the central road, with many more kilometers in the side trails. The back road cycling is good from either end: pleasant, easy pedaling over gently rolling hills. Riding south from PTH 44, the broad road chooses a winding route among dense jack pines. Pass under the double transmission line and take the turnoff to the south (right). Ride briefly past pastures, cross the train tracks, then swing to the east (left) to follow the road south towards PTH 15.

If you are cycling northward from PTH 15, explore the many side trails. Many peter out quickly, but two in particular merit investigation. The first well-defined trail heads off to the west (left), approximately 6 km north of PTH 15. Initially curving through sandy jack pine stands, the trail divides and disappears into a wall of vegetation: exploratory mountain bikers may yet find a route in to Julius Lake. The next major junction swings to the east (right), marked by a large boulder at the trailhead. Winding through fire-regenerated stands of jack pine, an excellent track gradually swings to the south. Although not confirmed by bicycle, this trail apparently returns to PTH 15, possibly traversing wet sections on the way.

Long distance marathoners could connect the trails of Agassiz and Sandilands Provincial Forests. The full distance from PR 214 to the Trans-Canada Highway creates 70 km of mountain bike tracks. Coast along the main artery as described above. Detour briefly along PTH 15 to the hamlet of Lewis. Follow the gravel south, across the old highway and the tracks, to where it connects with PR 506. Follow this road west, then south, across the Winnipeg Aqueduct and rail line to the Trans-Canada Highway and the maze of forestry roads and trails of Sandilands (p.166). The ride gently rolls past jack pine, spruce, and aspen. This route has not been checked by bicycle.

The Beaches and Belair Provincial Forest

One great long sand playground stretches along the eastern shore of Lake Winnipeg from Netley Marshes to Elk Island. Flocking here on hot summer Sundays is a long-time Manitoba tradition. Good mountain biking trails and roads also honeycomb this cottage playground. Supplement a day or a vacation at the beach with a little pedaling, or make the beach a great bonus for a day of mountain biking.

Cruise paved or gravel cottage roads or explore extensive trail networks. Good quality riding is there, but it can be patchy: some roads are short and congested, while some off road areas are plagued by extensive sand pits or very rutted gravel sections. If you hit poor riding conditions, try another trail and remember that there is a beach nearby. These are great hot weather trails, but the sand is a bonus for wet weather riding.

Type: Off road day rides; back roads and trails.
Access: Numerous locations via PTH 59, north of Patricia Beach. Lester Beach or Belair are suggested parking spots. Access to the trails in southern Belair Provincial Forest north of Stead, off PR 304; park near the junction of the new highway and the road leading south to Stead.
Facilities: Full facilities at Grand Beach and Stead. Limited facilities at other towns. No public facilities at many beach areas.
Distance: Unlimited choice of distances along beaches. Trails in southern Belair Provincial Forest over 15 km.
Difficulty: Easy to moderate (distances, hills, and surfaces).

Several specific areas are mentioned below, but the best advice is to explore. Use your cottage or any other selected location as a base and begin by investigating all the cottage roads, especially the ones along the edge of the forest. You will likely stumble across trails leading into the unknown, many used by trail bikes. Telephone or power lines are likely places for trails. Stick to well-traveled routes and the possibility of getting lost is remote; the area is completely surrounded by either water or PTH 59.

The largest trail network and the best surface (least sand) are located in the vicinity of the town of Belair, north of Grand Beach. Belair Provincial Forest extends north and south of the town and east of PTH 59. Trails radiate in all directions, but especially north of the main road. Some travel northeast to connect with recent cottage developments. One trail just west of the town runs

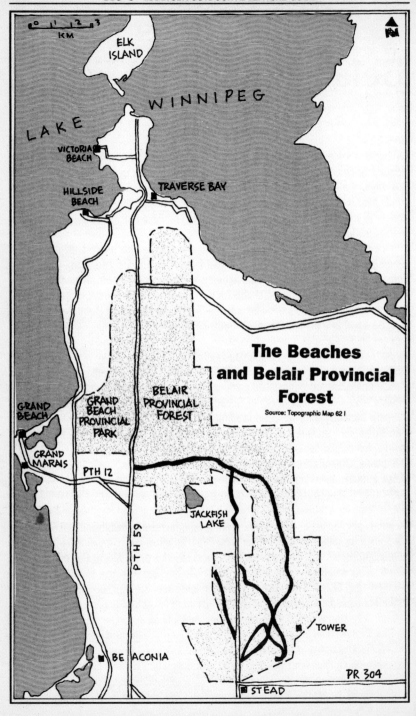

ELK ISLAND

L A K E — W I N N I P E G

VICTORIA BEACH

TRAVERSE BAY

HILLSIDE BEACH

GRAND BEACH

GRAND BEACH PROVINCIAL PARK

BELAIR PROVINCIAL FOREST

The Beaches and Belair Provincial Forest

Source: Topographic Map 62 I

GRAND MARAIS

PTH 12

PTH 59

JACKFISH LAKE

TOWER

BEACONIA

PR 304

STEAD

past the top of the provincial forest, rejoining PTH 59 near Albert Beach. The sandiness of this route has not been confirmed by bicycle.

The Lester Beach area also has some fine trails and many back roads to explore. Good trails with comparatively little sand extend from the community's northern edge. Find the telephone line leading north from First Street and use it as a main north-south artery for exploration. Side trails to the east (right turn) arrive at a gravel pit and further networks of trails. Going straight north, the trail crosses the Belair Road and briefly becomes Lowing Drive. Enjoy the downhill, then investigate the further series of delightful trails at the end of the road. Another trail leads north from the very southern edge of Lester Beach, running parallel to the main road, but its surface alternates between deep sand and 'washboard' gravel.

Cottagers in the Grand Beach, Grand Marais and Lester Beach areas also have easy access to the trails in Grand Beach Provincial Park. Many of the ski trails are not recommended for mountain biking: the hills are too steep and the swathes of sand too extensive.

It is possible to ride a mountain bike all the way from Beaconia to Victoria Beach. There are gravel roads and trails, and to some extent paved roads which could be explored, with the occasional refreshing plunge into the water. Add Elk Island to the itinerary in low-water years. Mountain bikers have been known to splash across the sand spits to the island.

Look for good family mountain biking in the southern end of Belair Provincial Forest. A small network of trails zigzags northeast towards a fire tower across largely level land. From the access, ride northeast (right) into the trees, ignoring the more traveled road due north. When it forks, select the most eastern road (to the right). This road leads to the fire tower. From the base there are good views to the east of the Brightstone Sandhills. Circle around just north of the tower and return to your car on the first road to the south. Cycle through most stages of forestry operations, from mature jack pines to clearcut areas, and patches of replanted pine. Several other trails mimic this basic route. Topographic map 62 I/8 is useful but not required for this area.

Riding very far north of the fire tower is not recommended: the roads sink into deeper and deeper sand, and are ridable only with difficulty. The same applies to the road leading from PTH 59 into Jackfish Lake in the central part of the forest. The pines are beautiful, but the sand is a nightmare. Southern Belair Provincial Forest could be reached directly on bicycle by riding the new highway leading off PTH 59 near Beaconia. This doesn't constitute very pleasant riding however, as the road is wide and the forest far from the roadsides.

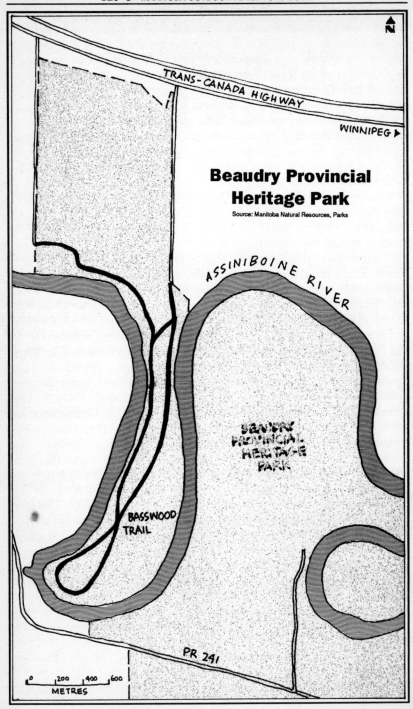

Beaudry Provincial Heritage Park

Source: Manitoba Natural Resources, Parks

Beaudry Provincial Heritage Park: North Bank

Just west of Winnipeg, Beaudry Provincial Heritage Park cradles long loops and bends of the Assiniboine River. The winter ice connects trails on both north and south banks, but without a summer link to the popular southern trails, those on the north bank see virtually no use. Leave the south bank trails for the hikers, and seek out the Basswood Trail by bicycle. Another north bank route, the Maple Trail, is difficult to access in the summer.

The Basswood Trail is especially recommended for families and cyclists just starting off road riding. There are no hills, although one of the access trails is a little rough. Cyclists looking for a longer ride can add extra kilometers by cycling the access roads or riding out from Winnipeg via PR 241 (p.49). The riverbank forest is magnificent, especially in autumn, but the trail and the access roads are very muddy after rain.

Type: Off road day rides; trails and back roads.
Access: Ride to north Beaudry from Winnipeg along PR 241, or transport the bikes to either of two unmarked gravel roads south from Trans-Canada Highway. The first access road is 5 km west of the weigh station at Headingley; look for the white building with small steeples on its roof. The second access is 6 km west of the weigh station. The road is not marked, but it is the last road to the south before St. Francois Xavier. Ride or drive to the dead end where the brown post marks the western boundary of the park.
Facilities: None. Nearest facilities in Headingley or St. Francois Xavier.
Distance: Up to 5 km.
Difficulty: Easy (distances, hills and surface).

From the first access, continue straight past the white building with steeples to the park gates and the northern end of the Basswood Trail. From the brown park posts of the most western access, follow the rough track eastward, skirting to the south of the cultivated field, along the river side. At the eastern end of the field a short trail leads into the forest, marked by a yellow sign indicating that hunting is not permitted. This trail quickly joins the Basswood Trail at its western end.

The Basswood Trail stretches in a figure eight along a deep meander of the river. The trail is occasionally marked by small yellow arrows, but its geographical location eliminates the possibility of getting lost. Spin along the level trails and enjoy the luxuriant growth and the river views. Basswood grows profusely along with American elms, aspens and Manitoba maple. The forest floor sports such specialties as riverbank grape and ostrich ferns. At the southern end of the trail there are two magnificent cottonwood trees. Here the trail slips down the miniature valley formed by meander scrolls of former river banks. Swing back to the north, past the point where the out-and-back trails squeeze together, and return to your starting point.

Birds Hill Provincial Park

Birds Hill Provincial Park has long attracted cyclists to its paved roads (p.25). The advent of the mountain bike brings a new type of cycling to Birds Hill. The park is a wonderful place to get a feel for off road riding, especially for families and beginners. The surface is good, there are no terrifying hills, and access is fast from Winnipeg. Enjoy many easy kilometers through Bird Hill's aspens, oaks, and meadows.

One major concern with off road riding at Birds Hill is conflict with other park users. Cross country ski and snowmobile trails are described below, but these are also popular with hikers and horseback riders. Watch for people and watch for horses. As with other provincial parks, but especially here, check with parks staff to get current information on trail closures. Then go out and cruise at anytime of the cycling season.

Type: Off road day rides; trails.
Access: Best access from Chickadee Trail parking lot, near Group Use Road on North Drive of Birds Hill Provincial Park. Alternative access from East or West Beach parking lots: cycle the bicycle path to the Group Use Road (p.27). Additional parking at stable. Note that bicycles may have to be lifted over gates across the trails in the vicinity of the stables.
Facilities: Latrines or washrooms, and water at trailheads. Snackbar and washrooms at stable. Campground in park.
Distance: Up to 60 km of trails as follows:

Chickadee Trail	4 km
White-tailed Deer Trail	10 km
Corral Trail	4.5 km
Ridge Trail	5 km
Lime Kiln Trail	5.8 km
Snowmobile Trails	30 km

Difficulty: Easy (easy to moderate distances; easy hills and surfaces).

The legacy of farming, logging and gravel extraction in Birds Hill is a vast network of roads, trails and paths across the park. Many of these are designated and maintained as cross country ski and snowmobile trails in the winter. The white fiberglass posts marking the ski trails remain in place all summer, but the snowmobile routes are marked only occasionally at junctions. The ski trails are signed for one way traffic, but cycle them from any direction in the

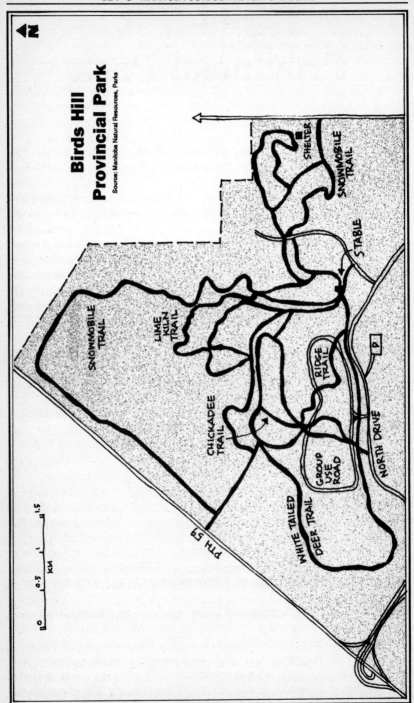

Birds Hill
Provincial Park
Source: Manitoba Natural Resources, Parks

summer. If you are following the direction of travel for skiing, look for posts with colored signs on your right; if you are going against the skiing direction, watch for the white post on the left. Most junctions are marked.

The easiest trails to follow are: the Chickadee Trail; the western half of the White-tailed Deer Trail; the Corral Trail, and the Ridge Trail.

The red Chickadee Trail leads north from the far end of the Chickadee parking lot. Across the Group Use Road, two paths diverge: out-and-back trails, which later converge. Follow either one through open forests and across the paved road of the Group Use Area a second time. Climb the hill to the viewing tower; this is an excellent area to practice a little hill technique. The Chickadee Trail swings further north in a loop starting and ending at the base of the tower.

The longer and flatter White-tailed Deer Trail extends west (to the left) from the Chickadee parking lot. Look for the trail near the latrines. Riding in this direction is against the skiing direction. Flashing in and out of open meadows and tall aspen groves, this broad, grassy old road curves and dips west, south then north and northeast. Pass the winter warm-up shelter, and continue further to the junction with the Chickadee Trail by a small gravel pit. One branch of the Chickadee Trail leads south (right) to the viewing tower, while a connection to the snowmobile trails heads northwest (left). Continue straight on the joint Chickadee and White-tailed Deer Trails to a second pit. The ski trails swing slightly to the right. In a tall aspen grove the Chickadee returns south to the right, while the White-tailed Deer continues straight east, later swinging down to the stable.

The short Corral Trail also originates from the Chickadee parking lot. Cycle either of two parallel tracks east (to the right) as they follow the gradual curve of the Group Use Road. There are a few gently rolling hills before the trails join the paved bicycle trail. Cruise the pavement to the stable, or select the more direct route along the Corral Trail which leads straight off from the paved path. Follow the telephone line back to the stable, swooping up and down a few gentle hills.

Ride the full loop of the Ridge Trail from the stable, or connect with this trail from the Group Use Road or the bicycle path. From the stable follow the joint trails, turning left at each of the two marked junctions. After the last junction the trail climbs slightly among bur oak. Ride the roller coaster hills, then tear down the one other big hill of the trails. Follow the climb back to the viewing tower hill. The route back to the stable zips past the warming shelter, then bops down a hill to cross the Group Use Road near the access road to Site 7. Wind among the Group Use Sites on the trail to emerge by the parking lot of Site 3. Follow the access road to the junction with the Group Use Road and the paved bicycle path.

North of the riding stable spreads a confusing welter of trails, old roads and open areas. The Lime Kiln Trail twists among the Ridge and White-tailed Deer Trails, and several snowmobile trails. The Lime Kiln is the trickiest trail to follow, as it passes through many open areas and half a dozen intersecting paths and roads. Head out, following the directional markers as well as you can, and experiment. One of the turns most readily missed is a sharp right hand turn soon after the lime kiln, across a very sandy stretch. Watch for horses in this area.

Several snowmobile trails reach into the northern and eastern corners of the park. Connect with the northern trail where it crosses the Lime Kiln Trail as a road. If you're heading north towards the lime kiln, turn east (right) onto the snowmobile trail. It will carry you south to a confusing junction of five trails. Find the one on the immediate left which heads west then north. The other trails lead to the Interpretive Workshop Road or to the stables. Further north, the snowmobile trail bumps up against the Lime Kiln Trail in an environment of open prairie, bur oak and aspen, and you may wander onto one or the other trail at this point. Further north along the snowmobile trail the trees close in, grading into dense spruce. With the spruce comes wet riding, especially in spring. The trail swings to the west and then south. Here it leaves the forest and follows PTH 59 across open fields. It's a long haul back to a sharp turn to the east and back into the trees. Take the turn to the north to follow the snowmobile route proper, or go straight to join the White-tailed Deer or Chickadee Trails.

Along the eastern boundary of the park and north of the stables, more snowmobile trails squiggle and turn. Enter the trails from the road to the Interpretive Workshop where a pair of trails cross the road. There are lots of twists and many T-junctions along this trail system, and several connections with PR 206. Although not checked by bicycle, it apparently is a pretty but confusing riding area. Arm yourself with a map and wander. Be very careful of horses here as these trails are used by riders, and the snowmobile trails also brush close to designated equestrian trails where you definitely should not be.

Brandon Hills

The Brandon Hills rise as a thin blue line running east to west just south of Brandon. The unique geomorphology and the thick cover of vegetation are protected in two blocks by the Brandon Hills Wildlife Management Area, with a strip of private land in between. Look for deer, and also for a system of circular cross country ski trails. These double as terrific mountain bike paths when the snow is off the ground. This was the site of the first mountain bike race in Manitoba, an event which has been repeated annually. The trail qualities which attract racers also appeal to recreational cyclists: variety of hills, good surface with little mud, swamp or sand, and choice of distances in a beautiful setting. This area ranks as a delightful ride in any cycling season. The grassy surface keeps the trail ridable, even after rain. Consider off road riding as a diversion from the Treesbank Circuit (p.105).

The ski trails are described below. Very fit cyclists may find these distances too short. The race course reaches into the eastern block of the Brandon Hills Wildlife Management Area, where the steepest inclines rise and the most challenging trails beckon. A confusing network of both maintained and overgrown trails snake up and down the hills. Unfortunately, reaching these trails requires crossing private land, and the trails themselves wind back and forth between public and private property. For this reason the eastern trails are not described here. Get a taste of the area by participating in the annual race. If you know someone acquainted with the local landowners, get permission and ride one of the most challenging mountain biking areas of Manitoba.

Type: Off road; trails.
Access: Turn off PTH 10, 10 km south of Brandon (antique store at corner). Travel 3.3 km west, turn south at first junction; travel 1 km and turn west into a parking area.
Facilities: None. Nearest full facilities in Brandon.
Distance: Four loops of 2.0, 2.5, 5.0 and 7.5 km.
Difficulty: Easy to moderate (easy distance and surface; moderate hills).

The ski trails at the Brandon Hills are arranged in three concentric loops which swing east and south of the parking area, plus the shortest circuit, to the west of the other trails. From the parking area, pass through the gate and continue straight to the main trails. Enclosed in oak and aspen forest, they are wide, smooth and conducive to fast spinning. The terrain is consistently hilly with some steep climbs, but most are neither very technical nor very arduous. If they do prove strenuous, rest at the convenient rustic benches.

Just past the gate the trail forks into two branches. The trail markers are

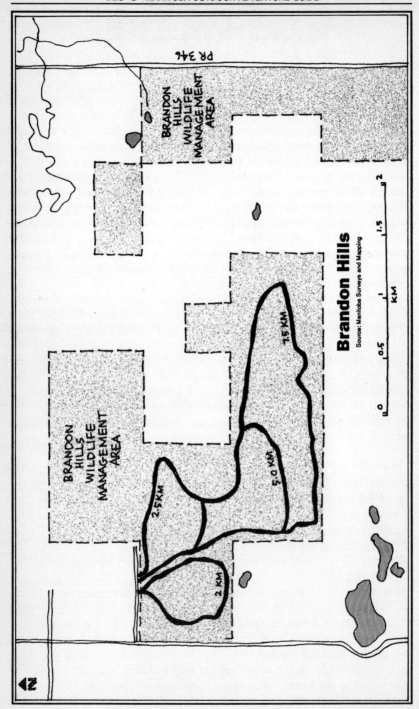

Brandon Hills

Source: Manitoba Surveys and Mapping

most obvious if you cycle counterclockwise, but the route below mimics the race course. Cycle straight from the gate, keeping the return trail to the south (right). Follow the jog of the trail to the south then the east (swing right then left), passing the warm-up cabin. Crank up and skim down the hills, passing two junctions to the east and south (both to the right), which connect with the 2.5 and 5 km trails. To cycle the full loop, ride straight or slightly to the left of these.

The overall direction of the trail veers to the south, then to the west, and then basically points straight north. At about the midway point, a trail to the east (left) heads towards private land and the eastern block of the Wildlife Management Area. Continue on the ski trail, zipping up and down hills. Pass the junctions of the two smaller trails from the east (but still on the right). The last few kilometers back to the parking area are a glorious, twisting runout on a fun, fast hill. Ride shorter circuits along the inner loops, or dip back and forth among the loops for greater variety. Connect with the shortest trail via a short spur through the aspens just before the return trail reaches the parking area gate.

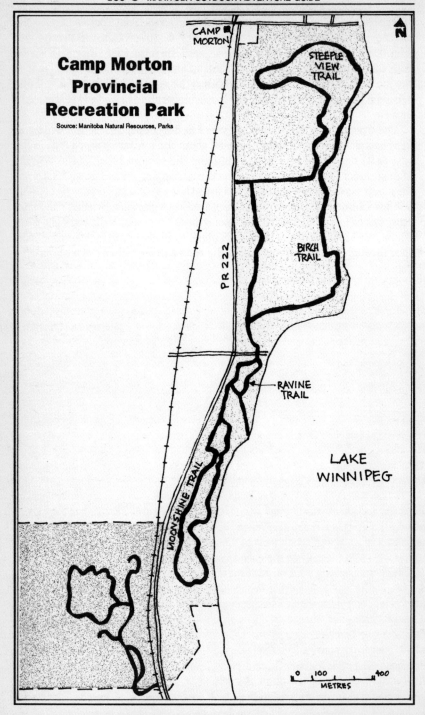

Camp Morton Provincial Recreation Park

Source: Manitoba Natural Resources, Parks

CAMP MORTON

STEEPLE VIEW TRAIL

PR 222

BIRCH TRAIL

RAVINE TRAIL

MOONSHINE TRAIL

LAKE WINNIPEG

0   100   400
METRES

Camp Morton Provincial Recreation Park

Camp Morton Provincial Recreation Park is a small but pretty refuge tucked along the western shores of Lake Winnipeg. The park preserves some of the loveliest lakeshore forests, featuring ash, elm, spruce, maple and oak. The level trails and few graded hills of the park suit it to families and those cyclists just starting off road riding. Check out the trails and trees in a day outing from the nearby towns and cottage areas. Combine cycling with a picnic, a swim, and a visit to the historical buildings in the memorial park to the north. Autumn is also a beautiful season to visit Camp Morton. Recent trail cutting has left a lot of cut twigs and short stumps on the trails, making pedaling a little harder, but this will improve with time. A few trails become slick when wet.

Type: Off road day rides; trails.
Access: Approximately 6.4 km north of Gimli. Turn east at McElheran Road, parking at road's end.
Facilities: None at parking area. Latrines, water, and picnic tables in park. Nearest full facilities in Gimli.
Distance: Trails total 7.7 km with individual trails between 1.3 and 2.8 km. Two roads totaling 1.5 km.
Difficulty: Easy (easy distances and hills; easy to moderate surface).

Four ski trails nestle tightly between Lake Winnipeg and PR 222, but they are not signposted in the summer. When the snow disappears, several other paths appear, including old roads west of the highway. Set off and explore; PR 222 to the west and the lake to the east exclude the possibility of getting lost.

From the parking spot on McElheran Road you can either ride north or south. To find the trails, cycle briefly west down the road to where the trails intersect. Zip over a wooden bridge to reach the southern and hilliest routes. The trail branches, then converges on a picnic area perched on a short cliff beside a small creek emptying into Lake Winnipeg. Daredevils can bounce and skid down earth stairs and balance across a log bridge. Alternately the stream can be forded near the mouth, or the whole area bypassed by finding the trail further to the west, in the ditch along PR 222. The Moonshine Trail further south was christened after a derelict still, found in a hollow of the trail. The trail consists of old roads and new trails with unexpected corners.

The trails north of the McElheran Road parking area are flat, with just two steep hills. The trees in this portion are magnificent, and these rides are exceptionally beautiful in the fall. Watch for stumps that grab your front tires, but also look for deer and bald eagles. A single track north of McElheran Road, the trail crosses a driveway before diverging into the Birch Trail loop. The eastern (right hand) trail leads to another picnic area set on a cliff, linked to PR 222 by a road. The continuation of the trail is presently hard to see at the northwest corner of the picnic area, because of the unmown grass in summer. The northern end of the Birch Trail travels west (left) along an old road. Slip back into the forest to the south (left) just before PR 222. It's easy to overshoot this turn. Continue straight south back to McElheran Road.

The newest trail, the Steepleview, comes within sight of the historic buildings further north, but doesn't connect directly. It swings in a tight loop at the northern end of the park. Join it from the northeast corner of the Birch Trail. Once on the Steepleview, it's easy to follow the twists back to the Birch Trail: there are no connecting roads or trails.

Add a few more kilometers by riding short roads in the forest west of PR 222. Access is south of McElheran Road: turn to the west from PR 222 at Lakeside Road. An old road is smooth, easy pedaling through the trees, while a circular road right-of-way is much rougher.

Duck Mountain Provincial Park and Forest

Duck Mountain Provincial Park and the surrounding forest in western Manitoba are a relatively unpedaled part of the province. Like its southern cousin, Riding Mountain, Duck Mountain offers backcountry day rides and touring along a multitude of back roads and trails. The landscape and vegetation feature prairies, mature forests and jack pine-aspen regeneration after forest fires. Many lakes are sprinkled liberally across rolling terrain, cut by river valleys.

Unlike Riding Mountain, backcountry cycling in Duck Mountain is not supported by designated trails and facilities. Most of the trails are old logging roads, used primarily today by hunters and fishermen. Many trails are long, some more than 40 km one-way. Ride circle routes in combination with municipal roads or gravel provincial highways. Families can find out-and-back rides to supplement hiking and fishing, but the park's greatest biking potential is for experienced mountain bikers with penchants for exploration.

PRs 367 and 366 traverse the park from east to west and from north to south, creating four large blocks of land. These are further dissected by the trails. Many are signed as Designated Vehicle Routes, but Parks does not maintain the roads, and some are rough going even for mountain bikes. Be prepared for mud, felled trees and beaver dams, and the almost constantly rolling hills. Expect the unexpected, which is all part of the fun.

Topographic maps 62 N/6, 62 N/7, 62 N/10, 62 N/11, 62 N/14 and 62 N/15 cover most of the area, showing details on lakes and elevations and some of the trails. Parks staff request that all backcountry users, especially overnight campers, register at park offices at Childs Lake, Blue Lakes or Wellman Lake; also notify them when you get back. There are no designated backcountry campsites for touring; camp where you wish but remember your wilderness etiquette and leave the site clean.

This is largely uncharted mountain bike country: be prepared with food, water, maps and tools. One route is described in detail below, with a few further riding suggestions. Follow your adventurous spirit, and select easy day trips, arduous marathons, or attach your panniers and tour the hills and lakes of Duck Mountain.

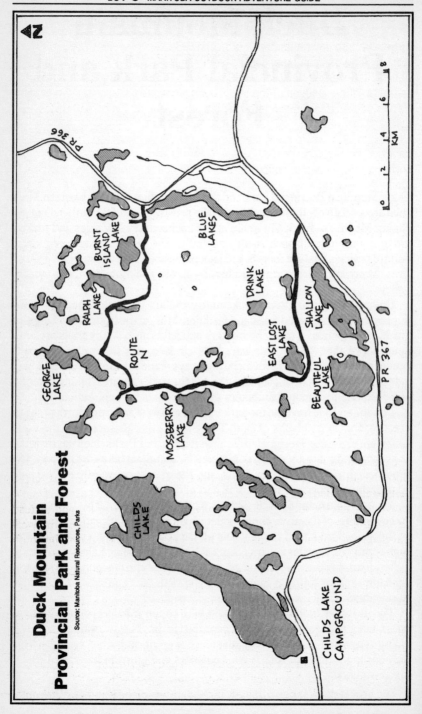

Duck Mountain
Provincial Park and Forest

Source: Manitoba Natural Resources, Parks

CHILDS LAKE CAMPGROUND

CHILDS LAKE

MOSSBERRY LAKE

GEORGE LAKE

ROUTE N

RALPH LAKE

BURNT ISLAND LAKE

BLUE LAKES

DRINK LAKE

EAST LOST LAKE

SHALLOW LAKE

BEAUTIFUL LAKE

PR 367

PR 366

KM

Designated Vehicle Route N

Type: Off road day rides; back roads and trails.

Access: The trail can be accessed from either PR 366 or PR 367. The best parking and starting point for the loop is from the Blue Lakes Campground just north of the junction of the two provincial roads.

Facilities: No facilities along trail. Full facilities at Blue Lakes and Childs Lake.

Distances: Vehicle Route N is approximately 32 km. Full loop from campground is approximately 38 km. Many side trails to explore.

Difficulty: Moderate to difficult (moderate to difficult distance and surface; moderate hills).

On the map, Designated Vehicle Route N appears as a gentle horseshoe in the center of the park. The first and third portions of the trip are fast-spinning fun, but the middle section degenerates considerably, with a very long beaver dam to tiptoe the bikes over. Altogether it offers a combination of challenge and pleasure that's hard to beat. Families or beginners can enjoy an out-and-back ride along the easier sections from either end of route N.

From the Blue Lakes Campground, cycle north on PR 366 to just past West Blue Lake. Turn west (left) to the broad dirt road, and zip down the first steep hill. Follow the main trail up the stiff climb to the southwest (left); the road to the north (right) soon ends near Marge Lake. Having conquered this climb, the terrain becomes gentler and you skim, rolling from the top of one hill to the next along a broad and good surface. Several wet spots where streams cross the road may slow you down, but even in a wet spring these are manageable. Cruise past the dense stands of jack pine and aspen, regrowing after the 1961 fire. Islands of white spruce and tamarack mark wetter areas which did not burn.

Several trails branch off the main route as it swings west, then north, past Burnt Island and Ralph Lakes, and on towards George Lake. Continue on the main, well-traveled road. The road clearly turns to the south. At the next major junction, leave the main trail which turns to the west (right), and instead choose the less traveled route to the south (left). (Continuing on the well-traveled road will take you towards Childs Lake.) A few km down the south trail you arrive at the shores of Mossberry Lake and an obvious campsite. Now the trail deteriorates, and large wet areas appear. Select the bypass routes, recently cut around the first few. For some, there is no easy solution except wet feet. The worst is the sprawling beaver dam. If there's an easy way to avoid this, it's not obvious. Teeter across the dam with bike in hand, then thrash your way through the brambles, over the jumble of logs, across the marshy grass and finally back to the main trail. Count on at least half an hour to get through this area. A few more obstructions are ahead, but once you've conquered this one the rest are easy (and you won't want to return this way!).

The beaver dam is approximately three-quarters of the way along the route.

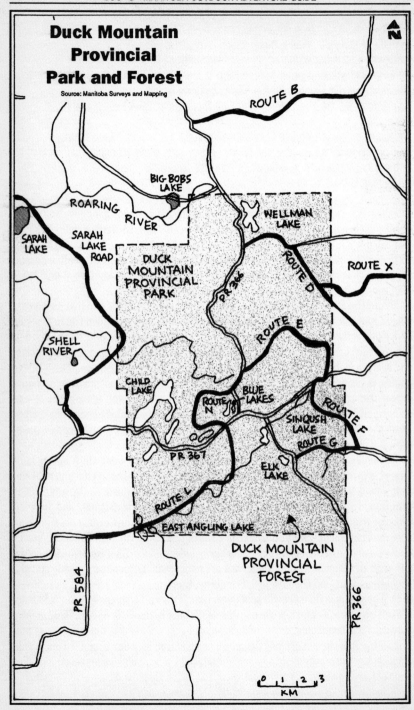

Duck Mountain Provincial Park and Forest

Source: Manitoba Surveys and Mapping

ROUTE B

BIG BOBS LAKE

ROARING RIVER

WELLMAN LAKE

SARAH LAKE

SARAH LAKE ROAD

ROUTE X

DUCK MOUNTAIN PROVINCIAL PARK

PR 366

ROUTE D

SHELL RIVER

ROUTE E

CHILD LAKE

BLUE LAKES

ROUTE N

SINGUSH LAKE

ROUTE F

ROUTE G

PR 367

ELK LAKE

ROUTE L

EAST ANGLING LAKE

DUCK MOUNTAIN PROVINCIAL FOREST

PR 584

PR 366

0 1 2 3
KM

Now it curves south then east skirting East Lost and Trapper Lakes, and ultimately back to PR 367. The route becomes increasingly well traveled, and the surface is good. Gallop up and down the frequent hills, splashing through the puddles waiting at the bottoms. Relish the rich forest of grand old spruces and mature poplars, unscathed by recent fires. For those riding the full loop, turn east (left) on PR 367, and enjoy the fast surface and long downhills to the junction with PR 366. Zip north (left) and back to the Blue Lakes.

Other Rides

Most of the other Designated Vehicle Routes in Duck Mountain are longer than Route N; however, out-and-back rides of any length can be ridden. Suggestions for rides along several designated routes are briefly outlined below to whet your exploratory appetite; they have not been confirmed by bicycle. Check the map for Game Hunting Area 18. There are no facilities along any of the routes, so come prepared.

Designated Vehicle Route G slashes across the southeast block of the park, from Elk Lake. It is generally a smooth surfaced, straight and dry route, with only a few wet obstacles. A loop of approximately 25 km can be ridden by following the wide road to the north (left) at the only major junction. This connects to the Sinqush Lake Campground. Return to Elk Lake via PRs 367 and 366.

The roads and trails in the southwest block of Duck Mountain (notably Designated Vehicle Route L) tend to be very wet. Route L passes East Angling Lake, and apparently connects with PR 584 and a network of hilly gravel roads.

To the northwest runs the big broad Sarah Lake Road, initially following the Shell River Valley, then climbing past the lakes and trees; it is over 40 km north to Sarah Lake and PR 586. The road quality degenerates further north, but is easily ridden by bike. At the southern segment of this road there is a major Y-junction within the Shell River Valley. The turn to the right leads to Sarah Lake; to the left is a connection with a network of trails through the forest north of Boggy Creek. Rather than swamps and beaver dams, some of these roads are plagued by sand.

Another trail in the northwest block is Designated Vehicle Route W. This picturesque route crosses the Roaring River, then visits Big Bobs Lake before continuing northwest to connect with PR 488. Exploring any of these routes would fill an enjoyable mountain biking holiday.

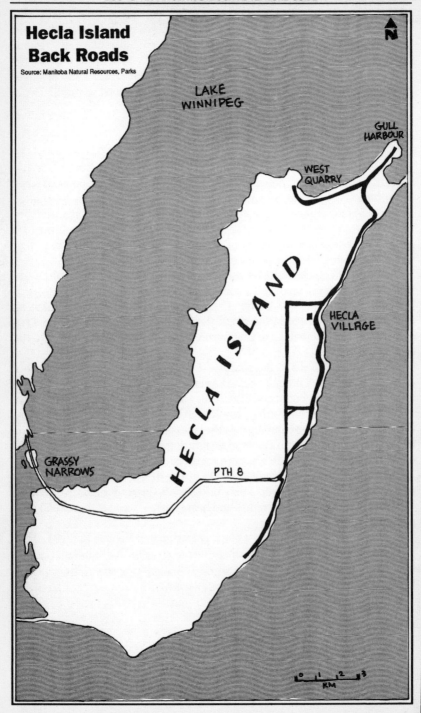

Hecla Island
Back Roads

Source: Manitoba Natural Resources, Parks

LAKE
WINNIPEG

GULL
HARBOUR

WEST
QUARRY

HECLA ISLAND

HECLA
VILLAGE

GRASSY
NARROWS

PTH 8

0 1 2 3
KM

Hecla Island Back Roads

In many ways Hecla Provincial Park is an aquatic preserve, with only islands and water enclosed within its boundaries. However, the connecting causeway has transformed the biggest island into an extension of the western shore of Lake Winnipeg. Hecla Island offers history and recreation in a stunning setting, and now off road riding can be added to the list of attractions.

For easy, pleasant cycling, Hecla Island ranks among the finest in the province. The landscape is level, the surface is smooth, and the scenery is a delightful blend of maritime and prairie elements. All cyclists can enjoy the riding here, from families looking for a short exploration to cyclists wanting to log a lot of scenic kilometers. Extend your paved road tour to Hecla (p.58) with off road variety. Two routes are described, a short trail at the northern end of the island, and a longer route along the eastern shore. Wet terrain limits further choice of trails. Enjoy off road riding in all seasons, but expect mud in spring and after rains.

The West Quarry Trail

Type: Off road day rides; back roads and trails.
Access: Start from Gull Harbor Resort or Campground at the northern extremity of Hecla Island. Trail signposted to the south of the resort parking lot and south of the campground.
Facilities: Full facilities at Gull Harbor. Latrines near west quarry.
Distance: 14 km return from Gull Harbor Resort.
Difficulty: Easy (easy distances, hills and surface).

From the main parking lot at the Gull Harbor Resort follow the trail through the trees, across the main road, past the campground, to the northern shore of the island. Here the trail broadens into an old road, scooting through stately trembling aspen, balsam poplar and white spruce. Watch for the interpretive signs about Hecla's moose population.

The trail emerges for the first good lake views near a small lagoon. Look across the bay to the trail's final destination, an old limestone quarry. The quarry itself is overgrown, but cabins and an icehouse remain from the fishing history of the island. At the trail's end, venture onto the spit and peer at the sunken boat in the harbor. Low limestone cliffs extend further west from the quarry, inviting exploration. The return is along the same trail; ignore other ski trails near the lagoon, which lead into swamps.

The Eastern Shore

Type: Off road day rides; gravel and back roads, with a short trail section.
Access: Start at either the Gull Harbor Resort and Campground, or at Hecla Village.
Facilities: Full facilities at Gull Harbor. Stores and B&B at Hecla Village. Latrines, water and picnic shelter at Group Use campground further south.
Distance: The longest route is 43.5 km return from Gull Harbor. Shorter routes possible, e.g. Gull Harbor to Hecla Village is 19 km return.
Difficulty: Easy to moderate (easy to moderate distances; easy hills and surface).

Icelandic settlement has been concentrated along the eastern shore of Hecla Island, and this ride blends natural and human history in a route from Gull Harbor south through Hecla Village and further along the eastern shore. Ride past pebble beaches and through thick forests, or past fishermen's houses set solidly on their lawns, staring over the water. Select loops of varying length, or ride short out-and-back trips.

Cycle from Gull Harbor to Hecla Village along the main road, cruising through luxuriant ash, maple, and aspen. Be careful of weekend traffic. Grab a glimpse of the water at the Quarry picnic site, where limestone cliffs rise jaggedly above the water. The road curves back into the trees, then returns to the shore and the turnoff to Hecla Village. From here, the scenery becomes very picturesque, and the traffic diminishes.

Historic Hecla Village stretches in a narrow, open line along the shore, each house facing out to the lake. An excellent self-guiding trail loops through the central portion of the village, recounting the story of this Icelandic community founded in 1876; a brochure is available with further details.

Cycling south from Hecla Village, the road hugs the low shoreline and more houses are passed, some deserted, others well-maintained. Follow the main road to where it curves sharply to the west. For a different return to Hecla Village or Gull Harbor, follow this road to the junction with PTH 8, and turn north (right). This newly completed section of road cuts across the center of the island for 7 km before reaching the northern end of Hecla Village. Presently gravel, this section of the road is slated to be paved by 1991.

For a longer tour, ride south from Hecla Village and follow the curve westward only briefly, then take the dirt road leading off to the southeast (left). This is more of a two-lane track than a road, and is the start of some superb back road exploring. For 2 km the trees begin to mingle with the open shoreline, and a few more structures are passed before a large Group Use campground is reached.

South of the group use area, the track dwindles to an overgrown trail through the forest. There are logs to hop, ruts to avoid, saplings to swerve around, but persevere. The worst section is just before the trail opens up into a road again: construction has partially obliterated the trail with a mound of earth, now grown-over with thistles. But this is momentary, and the reward is only a few pedal turns away.

Once again a high quality track appears, running between rich forests and low cliffs over rock beaches. Watch for grouse in the woods, grebes on the shore, and bald eagles overhead. Skim past several abandoned homesteads, a log cabin and an active fishing camp, before reaching an old homestead in a large, open field, 4 km from where the road reappeared. Three trails (designated vehicle routes) branch out from the open field around the campsite, marked by yellow signs. The adventurous could experiment with these trails, but the riding quality deteriorates sharply, with the trails overgrown and often wet.

Return by backtracking along the lakeshore road. Follow the curve of the road to the west (left), instead of continuing straight on the overgrown trail. Where it joins the main highway, turn north (right), and skim 9.5 km back to Hecla Village or 18 km back to Gull Harbor.

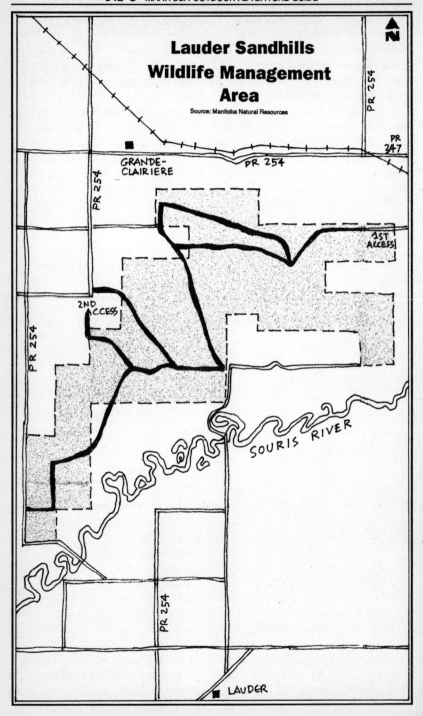

Lauder Sandhills Wildlife Management Area

Source: Manitoba Natural Resources

Lauder Sandhills Wildlife Management Area

The Lauder Sandhills are one of several areas in western Manitoba sculpted by sand from the glacial period. This is marginal agricultural land, but excellent habitat for white-tailed deer. The land has been set aside as a Wildlife Management Area (WMA), and mountain bikers have also benefited from the designation of the Lauder Sandhills as public land.

A network of roads and trails crisscross the Lauder Sandhills WMA, adding up to many kilometers of delightful riding. The hills are short but frequent, the crests of hidden dunes. The trail surface is excellent, with only occasional patches of deep sand to slow your tires. Wide enough to permit side by side riding, the trails twist and turn, creating a sense of tremendous variety. The Lauder Sandhills WMA has appeal for everybody, from easy exploring for families and recreational cyclists, to many fast training kilometers for racers. Consider exploring the Lauder Sandhills as a day off from the paved road riding of the Mouse and Turtle Tour (p.36). The sandy soils make this a good choice for wet weather riding, and the trails are particularly delightful in late spring when the cacti are blooming.

Type: Off road day rides; back roads and trails.
Access: Several roads and trails enter the WMA, located west of Hartney, but many require crossing private land. Easiest access is to travel west on PR 347 from PTH 21, to the junction with PR 254. Travel south for 1.6 km; to the west is the start of the WMA trails. Park along the road. A second suggested access is at the western edge of the WMA. Follow PR 254 past Grande-Clairiere and through its first, then second turn to the south. At 1.6 km after the second turn, turn east, and follow this road for about 2 km into the WMA, to where it starts to curve to the southeast.
Facilities: None. Nearest full facilities in Hartney on PTH 21.
Distance: Large network of trails allows selection of varied rides.
Difficulty: Easy to moderate (distances, hills and surface).

The trails in the Lauder Sandhills WMA tend to run east-west, with a few cutting diagonally across the WMA. Any number of out-and-back rides or loops can be enjoyed. Ride further kilometers and circle routes in combination with the adjacent municipal roads.

From the northeastern access, an easy loop can be ridden in the top portion of the WMA. Stick with the main trail while riding west, avoiding any junctions to the south (left). The trail whisks through aspen and bur oak, and across patches of open prairie, ending in a T-junction with a dirt road. Travel briefly south (left), passing the dump, then follow the trail as it leads off to the southeast. Where it soon branches, take the most northern trail (left), and follow it back to where it joins the main trail that you started on. Keep to the left to return to the start.

From the western access, skim along the wide road to the southwest. Swatches of prairie cut through the aspen and oak. There are several easy loops from this trail. Veer to the west (right), then to the northwest (right again) to emerge by a field. Follow the edge of the quarter section north then east (2 right turns), to return to the start.

For another loop, follow the trail from the western access further east, to the junction with the municipal road. Take the trail to the north (left), and follow this intimate trail northwest to the dump, then due west back to PR 254. Some of the sandhills along this route have been exposed by dirt bike traffic. Turn south (left) to the start. An alternate return from the municipal road at the southeast corner of the WMA is along the gravel roads to the south, west, then north (all right turns), flitting across the Souris River twice.

Set out and explore the other trails of the WMA. The WMA is surrounded by private land, and while the distinction between public and private is sometimes difficult, respect the latter. In particular there is no public access to the Souris River. Stay on the trails in the WMA both to protect the prairie ecosystem and to avoid the spines from the pincushion and prickly pear cacti which could deflate your fat tires.

Northern Off Road

In one sense, off road possibilities in northern Manitoba seem limitless; in another they are very constrained. The amount of land boggles the mind, and logging and mining activities have punched many roads through the landscape. However, many lead into treeless clearcuts and others dissolve in swamps or lakes. The best maintained roads are those in active use, and they may be private. Off road adventurers in northern Manitoba should pour over maps, talk to local hunters or fishermen, and check with the logging and mining companies. An example of the possibilities are two roads south of Cranberry Portage. Athapap Road heads west from PTH 10, and trails connect the road to Athapapuskow Lake. Simonhouse Road beckons to the east from PTH 10, heading towards Simonhouse Lake. These have not been checked by bicycle. Exploring these back roads extends a northern cycling holiday (p.41).

Rock and water also preclude cycling on many of the northern ski trails. An exception is the cross country ski trail system at Clearwater Lake Provincial Park, near The Pas. Hilly and challenging, a network of 22 km of ski trails is tucked between PR 287 and cottage roads. The hills may be overwhelming for some cyclists; practice first on the area's gravel roads, then explore the pedaling pleasures of the ski trails. The trails are being extensively upgraded over several years; there will be removal of rocks and roots, increases to the height of the hills, and surfacing with woodchips (check with Manitoba Natural Resources in The Pas regarding the latest trail conditions). These changes will improve riding under all weather conditions, but in the interim expect water, wet moss, and mud on the trails close to the lake.

Type: Off road day rides; trails and back roads.
Access: Several roads or trails lead into the ski trail network. The easiest access is to follow the cottage road off PR 287 along Pioneer Bay. Park at the dead end; a trail leads directly south, away from the water. Two alternate starting points are to continue east on PR 287, past the Pioneer Bay turnoff. Select either of the two trails or roads leading north (left turn). The second road is the unmarked access to the ski chalet.
Facilities: None at trailheads or along trails. Stores, snacks and accommodation at lodges in Clearwater Provincial Park. Camping and picnic facilities with water at several sites in park. Full facilities in The Pas.
Distance: Over 22 km, with approximately one third of the trails west of the chalet, and two thirds east of the chalet.
Difficulty: Moderate (easy to moderate distances and surface; moderate to difficult hills).

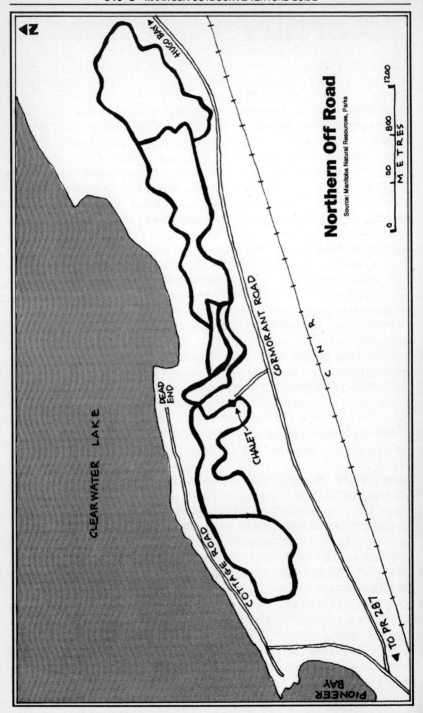

Northern Off Road

Source: Manitoba Natural Resources, Parks

The cross country ski trails at Clearwater Lake Provincial Park stretch in elongated loops by the shore of Clearwater Lake. Although many are short, the cluster of trails in this compact area can temporarily confuse cyclists, especially as the trails are not fully signposted in summer. This wedge of land is entirely enclosed by the lake and gravel roads, eliminating the possibility of getting lost. Use the map and directions as a rough guide for your explorations. The map produced by The Pas Orienteering Club shows a few more topographic details for the western half of the trails.

The road south from the dead end of the cottage road divides the ski trails in half. Cycling south along the road, a trail leads into the conifers to the west (right). Follow it through the dampness to where it ends in a T-junction. To the southeast (left) takes you to the chalet, but choose the trail up the hill to the northwest (right). Climbing hard, veer to the north (right), and follow the curves of the trail, rising still more. Catch your breath as you coast through the spruces, before plunging back down the ridge to the north. At the bottom several trails diverge to the north and south. The northern ones (right side) lead quickly to the cottages and the lake. Several trails lead back up the cliff. Select the third and least arduous one. At the top, take the trail to the west (right), which swings in a crooked loop back to the east. Several trails branch to the right as you ride counterclockwise, leading to more cottages.

Heading east, the trail encounters an old road. Turn north (left), soon taking the trail to the east (right). Follow its twists. Just before the chalet the trail forks, and these branches then fork repeatedly. Feel your way around the trails to reach the gravel pit at the side of the chalet. There are some steep descents here. If you find yourself among the conifers at the bottom of the ridge with no sign of the chalet, turn south (right) at any junction, which should carry you back up to the gravel pit.

Myriad trails also crisscross and branch in the eastern half of the ski trail system, and these trails tend to be wetter, especially close to the lake. The limestone ridge continues through the eastern trails, with level riding at the top and bottom of the ridge, and stiff climbs in between. Cycling south from the dead end of the cottage road, ride past the access trail to the western system. Two trails diverge to the east (left) soon after. The first one zips past old cabins to the lakeshore, while the second one climbs slightly, then reaches a T-junction. Turn east (left) on this second trail and cycle straight, ignoring all intersecting trails. In less than a kilometer, the first trail joins from the north (left). Scoot along for the next two kilometers, ignoring any trails to the south (right). Just past a warming hut the trail can be followed further east to a Boy Scout camp near Hugo Bay. To return on the ski trail system, ignore this turn and swing south, then head to the west. Twist with this main trail, continuing past any junctions, emerging on the gravel access road leading to the chalet. Ride north, and find the trails leading from behind the chalet. Zip down to the bottom of the ridge and veer to the northeast (right) to find the route back to the parking area at the dead end cottage road.

Off Road in Towns and Cities

Off road adventuring begins at home. The majority of Manitobans and of mountain bike owners live in the towns and cities of the province. Many use their mountain bikes to commute to work, or for Sunday riding around streets and bike paths. If you view the upright handle bars and fatter tires as a convenient substitute for your road bike, off road exploring in your home town or city adds a new dimension to cycling. Experiment at home, and then check out trails near your cottage or favorite camping area. Go on to explore further delights of off road riding in Manitoba. For those already attracted to the backwoods potential of mountain bikes, use town and city riding to build skills which will improve your riding on the tougher trails. A lot of good training hours can be logged from your back door.

Riding from your back door is the greatest advantage of seeking out unknown corners of urban Manitoba. No car racks, no wheel removals, just set out and ride. The price for this convenience includes fewer trails, fewer challenges, dealing with vehicle traffic, and no sense of wilderness or 'getting away from it all'. For most people, out-of-town riding is only an option on the weekend, and during the week the home town or city still offers exercise and fun.

Whether you live in Winnipeg, Portage la Prairie, Brandon, The Pas, or any other Manitoba community, the places to look for off road riding are the same. Start with bike paths or designated bicycle routes (e.g. in Winnipeg and Brandon). Where the pavement ends, the trails often begin. Parks are usually crisscrossed with paths and are a great place to get the feel of off road terrain. Respect other park users and any signs prohibiting bicycles. Cross country ski trails (except when they are on golf courses) are often great riding, for example, the Crescent Park trails in Portage. Two parks outside Winnipeg deserve special mention. La Barriere Park to the southwest and Little Mountain Park to the northwest are excellent locations to build off road confidence. La Barriere snakes along the La Salle River, offering a network of trails and good hills to practice your climbing and to overcome any downhill fears. Little Mountain Park is absolutely flat, but has myriad easy riding trails. Both parks are very popular with walkers, and La Barriere becomes very muddy after rain or in the spring.

Many Manitoba towns and cities are built on rivers, and the banks are often a source of trails and sometimes the best hills. The riverbank trails around Assiniboine Park in Winnipeg are short but wonderful. Search out any other hills. Try rehabilitated landfills, or gravel pits. Abandoned rail lines can sometimes be found. In Winnipeg one runs west, just north of the junction of Cathcart Road and Wilkes Avenue.

A final suggestion is to check out the edge of town, where the paved roads are replaced by gravel roads. These are the next best thing to off road, and exploring them may lead to more trails. In Winnipeg, check out the southwest corner of the city. Cycle south from the Assiniboine Park and Forest along McCreary Road, towards the Fort Whyte Nature Centre. The gravel road network takes you west then north, connecting with the rail line. The floodway curves to the east of the city and although flat, provides many kilometers of off road riding. In Portage, cross the Assiniboine and explore the roads from PR 240 along the river. Brandon residents can also explore riverside gravel roads; the Treesbank Circuit (p.105) heads out along some of these. Get on your bike and ride, and with a little imagination, off road trails will appear. Have fun!

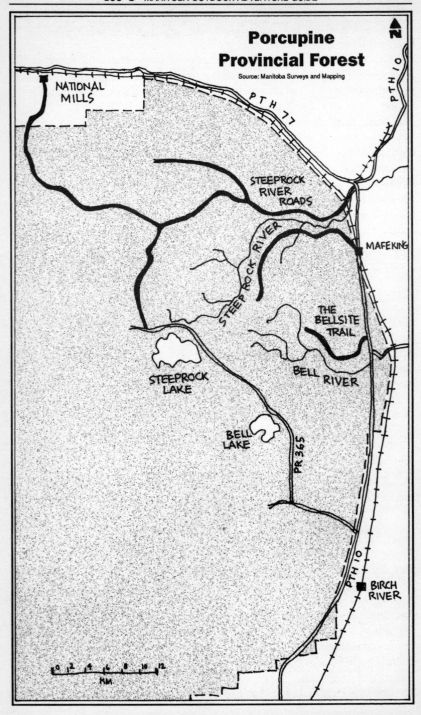

Porcupine
Provincial Forest

Source: Manitoba Surveys and Mapping

N

PTH 10

PTH 77

NATIONAL MILLS

STEEPROCK RIVER ROADS

STEEPROCK RIVER

MAFEKING

THE BELLSITE TRAIL

BELL RIVER

STEEPROCK LAKE

BELL LAKE

PR 365

PTH 10

BIRCH RIVER

0 2 4 6 8 10 12
KM

Porcupine Provincial Forest

Porcupine Provincial Forest is known among fishermen and hunters, but mountain bikers have yet to discover the hills and thrills of the northern end of the Manitoba Escarpment. Rising steeply from the plains, Porcupine has the steepest rides in the province. Even at the 'top,' the terrain changes to rolling hills which continue a gradual rise westward, graced by trees and lakes, logging roads and trails. This is a part of Manitoba where bears, moose and elk figure strongly in local conversations.

The trails in Porcupine Provincial Forest are not limitless. Three are suggested here which focus on the wall of the escarpment. Exploratory cyclists may discover trails on the top, but swamps and lakes limit cycling possibilities, and many logging roads traverse clearcut areas or are actively used by logging companies. Be wary of cycling PR 365 into North Steeprock Lake: it's dominated by thundering logging trucks and cars with swaying trailers. Some of the forests at the top of the escarpment have been recently burned, but nonetheless Porcupine Provincial Forest is beautiful and well worth exploring.

Porcupine is for experienced cyclists, and a good fitness level increases the pleasures of the steep climbs. Topographic map 63 C/11 is useful for general orientation, but parts of the suggested routes do not appear. The roads up the escarpment remain ridable even after heavy rain, and can be conquered at any time of the cycling season.

The Bellsite Trail

Type: Off road day rides; back roads.
Access: The trailhead is off PTH 10, although the turnoff is not marked. Turn west (left) approximately 2 km north of the junction to Bellsite. It passes initially through a gravel pit and a pine plantation. There is no particular parking area; just ensure that the trail is not blocked.
Facilities: No facilities along trail. Nearest full facilities in Birch River.
Distances: Approximate one way distance to top is 11 km. Trails continue at top for an unknown distance.
Difficulty: Difficult (moderate distance; difficult hills and surface).

The Bellsite Trail is tough, but the scenery and the reward at the top are wonderful. The trail climbs the steepest and highest face of Porcupine Provincial Forest, and the elevation gain in 5 km is estimated at 336 m (1200 ft). A telling indicator of effort is the travel time: one and a half hours to go up and 15 minutes to come down! Come and try it!

The trail is in fact a road, but is passable only by four-wheel drive vehicles. After the turnoff from PTH 10, the trail curves south and then swings west. There is one junction near the beginning; take the road to the left. Thereafter stick to what is clearly the main road, ignoring a few fire breaks and bush trails.

The trail begins easily, the first kilometer enticing you with gentle rises and fast spinning through aspen forest. Then the climb begins. Ascend the escarpment in a series of short (and not so short) steep climbs interspersed with either small downhills or brief level sections. Some of these hills require both stamina and technical skill to reach the top without getting off and pushing. It is generally a dry, well-drained route, but in a wet spring expect patches of mud and an eroded and rough surface. Throughout the climb you are enclosed in dense mixed forests, and the only rewarding views are at the top. From there it is possible to see the north basin of Lake Winnepegosis. Picnic and rest among the replanted pines. The trail at the top continues to the west to a fire tower, but has not been checked by bicycle. The ride back down to the trailhead is fast and exhilarating: check your brakes, then hang on and enjoy.

Steeprock River

The Steeprock River Valley is an intriguing and remote corner of Manitoba. The Steeprock River has carved steep canyons into the rise of Porcupine Mountain, and the steepness of the valley walls have preserved them from logging. Under consideration for a provincial wilderness park, the area is devoid of facilities. Although not checked by bicycle, it is reportedly as rugged and grueling as the Bellsite Trail.

The Steeprock River Valley is best accessed by an unmarked dirt road approximately 1.6 km north of Mafeking on PTH 10. There is apparently a small network of trails; follow the road that goes most directly west. The road climbs gradually, then very steeply, with magnificent canyon views. The road may continue on the top, although the area receives little traffic apart from the occasional trout fisherman. Consider this route for an exciting exploratory day ride in stunning scenery.

A longer, but less remote and scenic ride is found just north of the Steeprock River. An all-weather road cuts across the northern end of Porcupine, with connections to Steeprock Lake and National Mills, close to the Saskatchewan border on PTH 77. To access this road, travel north of Mafeking on PTH 10, and turn west (left) onto PTH 77. Just after this junction, turn south (left) near the rail line. The road heads south initially, then swings west onto a good quality road before scaling the escarpment. Near the crest there is a junction with the road to the right leading to the Rice Lake fire tower: however, views of the Steeprock River are apparently limited. Long distance tours could be ridden on this road but there are no designated facilities. This road has not been checked by bicycle.

Riding Mountain National Park

Riding Mountain National Park is a mountain biking wonderland. Extensive trail systems, stunning scenery, and the opportunity to view wildlife are among its many assets. Probably the best known off road area in the province, it is certainly the best organized, with designated biking trails and a descriptive trail map. Of the 33 trails in the park, 9 can be cycled and are described here. Choices range from easy day rides to extended camping trips in the central and western portions of the park. The trails are listed below in order, east to west across the park.

The scenery is as varied as the trails. The Birdtail Valley winds across the western end of the park, while the Manitoba Escarpment sharply defines the eastern boundary. In between, lakes nestle and hills roll through dense spruce forests, elk prairies and bright deciduous groves. Every season seems special in Riding Mountain; plan a trip around seasonal wildlife activities or when forest or prairie flowers are blooming.

Many of the designated cycling routes are former fire roads or warden patrol routes, and are broad, with an easy-pedaling surface. Few trails offer technical challenges. Some of the trails are muddy after heavy rains; check with Visitor Services or the wardens on current trail conditions. The national park status bars motorized vehicles from the routes, and there is no hunting season. Camping is only permitted in designated campsites, and a camping permit must be obtained in advance from the Information Centre, the North or South Gates, or any warden station (pick up the excellent park trail map while you're there). Inform the parks officials when you leave. Full facilities are only found in Wasagaming.

Combine off road riding inside the park with the extensive gravel road network to the south (p.101). Celebrate completion of a paved road tour around Riding Mountain National Park (p.54) by exploring remote corners away from traffic.

North Escarpment Trail

Type: Off road day rides and tours; back roads and trails.
Access: Two access points from the south: across PR 19 from Dead Ox Creek picnic site; or the gated road just west of the Beaver Pond Exhibit on PR 19 (limited parking). Three pick-up points along northern end of trail. The

first is on PR 361, west of McCreary. To reach the second, follow PR 480 west from Laurier to its turn north. Turn south (left) instead, passing 2 mile-roads, then turn west (right) again and travel to the park boundary. The third pick-up is at the Ochre River trailhead. Directions for this pick-up are complex, and Parks Canada staff suggest checking at the East Gate or the Information Centre for detailed instructions.

Facilities: Latrines and picnic tables at Dead Ox Creek, and latrines and water at the Deep Lake, Scott Creek, and Noisy Creek campsites.

Distance: To the top of the Agassiz Ski Hill is 13 km one way. Full trail to Ochre River pick-up is 53 km one way.

Difficulty: First 10 km easy; remainder of trail difficult.

Despite an easy beginning, the North Escarpment Trail is the most rugged and technically demanding trail which is open to cyclists in the park. The trail initially rides high on the escarpment, then plunges down its eastern slope, and ends by picking its way along the base to the north. It is a long trail, parts of which could be done in day trips, either out-and-back or with pre-arranged pick-up. Tours could take advantage of the Scott Creek and Noisy Creek campsites on the northern half of the trail. Parks Canada is planning to stop maintaining the northern end of the trail and the Noisy Creek campsite, and riding quality may deteriorate in a few years.

The access on PR 19 just west of the beaver pond is recommended. Sail north from the gate on the first 9 km of easy pedaling along the wide, gravel road. In 1980 a fire swept through this area leaving it bare and open, but now the trees are growing back, providing valuable habitat for bear, elk and moose. Just 1.6 km down this road, the other access trail joins. Further on the road forks at a spruce regeneration plot. The road to the east (right) called the Jet Trail is a great diversion leading to a stupendous view. Back at the junction, follow the main road to the west of the spruce plot. Pass the highest point in the park (756 m) after 5 km of pedaling. One km further is the turnoff to the bumpy, steep, but short trail to the Deep Lake campsite.

After the Deep Lake turnoff the road curves to the east and then to the south, descending gradually. With a sharp turn to the north it narrows and becomes overgrown until it is reduced to a track. The trail follows the edge of the escarpment for 3 km, emerging near the top of the Agassiz Ski Hill. Before teetering over the edge, admire the view and check your brakes, then hang on for the screaming descent. Wind through the aspens, ford McKinnon Creek, and emerge from the forest on PR 361. Return in a full circle to the start by choosing gravel roads heading south, parallel to PTH 5. Turn west (right) onto PR 19 and climb the switchbacks to the parking area.

The North Escarpment Trail continues north past PR 361 along the base of the hills. Work your way along the flat trail, through dense deciduous forest, crossing an occasional stream. At the next junction, take the east branch (right) to the middle pick-up point or pedal on to the northeast and towards the Noisy Creek campsite. Near the end, the trail swerves sharply to the north before joining the Ochre Creek Trail. Turn east (right) and follow it to emerge at the pastures and the pick-up point.

Muskrat Lake Trail

Type: Off road day rides; back roads.
Access: Two parking areas: at trailhead proper, 8 km south from PR 19 on Rolling River Road; or for a longer ride, at trailhead for Rolling River Fire Self-guiding Trail, just off PR 19 (then cycle the 8 km to the trailhead).
Facilities: Latrines at Rolling River Self-guiding Trail on PR 19. No facilities at trailhead or along trail.
Distance: From trailhead proper, 12 km one way; from Rolling River Fire Trail, 20 km one way.
Difficulty: Easy to moderate (distance, hills and surface).

The Muskrat Lake Trail carries mountain bikers into the southeast corner of Riding Mountain National Park. This is an area of ecological contrasts, including the stark snags and lush regrowth from the 1980 forest fire, islands of unscathed spruce and jack pine, and grass-covered hills between low-lying meadows.

This is an out-and-back ride: the intersecting trails are not designated as cycling trails. The destination is the old Kelwood fire tower site. If the farthest parking lot is the chosen start, it's a fast and easy spin south along the broad gravel road to the trailhead. The trail begins in a low-lying area, and soon crosses a shallow tributary of the Rolling River. Skim along the old fire road, which swings southeast then due east across gently rolling topography. About halfway, the road crosses a high point from which the folds of the escarpment can be seen. The junction with the South Escarpment Trail (the 'Four Corners') is just a few turns of the crank further. The remaining 5 km are cleared only infrequently, but are ridable. Rest at the fire tower site, then retrace your tracks back to the starting point.

Grey Owl Trail

Type: Off road day rides; trails.
Access: Turnoff to parking lot 1 km east of PTH 10, on north side of PR 19.
Facilities: Latrines at trailhead and at Grey Owl's Cabin.
Distance: 18 km return.
Difficulty: Easy to moderate (easy distance; moderate hills and surface).

A pleasant pedal through aspen-spruce forests and beside lakes and ponds, this trail leads to a log cabin briefly inhabited by Grey Owl, an Englishman turned conservationist in the guise of an Indian. The trail is one of the few designated cycling routes in the park which is not a road, and along the first few kilometers rocks and roots must be negotiated. However the technical challenges are not great, and this trail is recommended as a day trip for riders of all abilities.

Head out from the parking lot through thick spruce forest. After winding tightly through the trees, follow the arrow and take a right turn at the junction. For the remainder of the ride the trail is comfortably wide, with fewer rocks and roots. The trail is well signposted, and at the various junctions travel distances are provided. Continue north past the junction of the Kinosao Lake Trail, and the turnoff to the Cowan Lake Trail. The final kilometers skirt beaver ponds hedged by black spruce, and may be wet. After 8.5 km the trail arrives at Beaver Lodge Lake where the cabin stands. Retrace your route back from Grey Owl's Cabin. For a little variety, follow the signs for the Kinosao Lake Trail back to the parking area.

Strathclair Road

Type: Off road day rides or tours; back roads.
Access: Trailhead and parking at north end of the bison enclosure.
Facilities: None at trailhead. Two primitive campsites along trail, with latrines and water.
Distance: 23 km one way.
Difficulty: Moderate (moderate distance and hills; easy surface).

The Strathclair Trail runs north from the bison enclosure to the northern park boundary, tracing the valley of the Vermilion River. You don't often see the river, just occasional views of folded hills around a deep valley. Originally a settler road traveled by horse and wagon, the two ruts of the trail provide an excellent surface for fast spinning. Reasonably fit cyclists can ride the Strathclair Trail as a pleasant day trip, or it can be considered for a very easy overnight tour.

Head out from the bison enclosure, and at the fork, take the trail to the north (right). The first few kilometers pass through grassy elk meadows, bordered by aspen and spruce forests. The occasional solitary spruce shows off a magnificent size and shape.

Pass the turnoff for the Kinnis Creek campsite after 8 smooth km. The hills are more pronounced in this section: whiz down the steep descents to cross tributary creeks of the Vermilion River. You may chance upon elk, moose or even a bear along this stretch. Consider a picnic lunch at the Vermilion River campsite, or ride a further 5 km to the end of the trail. Descend the long, gradual hill to the Vermilion River Warden Station. When you're rested and well fed, turn around, climb up through the aspens, then skim up and down the hills and across the meadows back to the bison enclosure and the start.

The Central Road

Type: Off road day rides or tours; back roads.
Access: Eastern access at bison enclosure; western access at either Deep Lake Warden Station or further north near Bob Hill Lake, where a gate bars vehicle traffic. Parking at both areas.
Facilities: None at trailheads. Several primitive campgrounds along route with latrines and water.
Distance: Total one-way distance from the bison enclosure to the Deep Lake Warden Station is 73 km. Many connections with other trails.
Difficulty: Easy to difficult (easy to difficult distance; easy to moderate hills and surface).

The central road runs like a backbone from the middle of the park out to its western end. This broad, easy-riding road forms the foundation for many varied mountain bike trips in Riding Mountain. Frequent trails branch off, and campsites dot the entire length. This is the best that the province has to offer for long-distance off road riding. Alternately, eat up the kilometers in a day ride from Lake Audy. Ride out to a campsite along the Central Road, then explore the nearby trails unencumbered on day trips. When coupled with the gravel roads south of the park (p.101), the possibilities for fat tire touring become endless.

The Central Road is also popular with hikers and horseback riders, causing some competition for the campsites. Remember to obtain a backcountry camping permit. Although generally a good surface, the section between Baldy Lake Road and 5 km west of Gunn Creek campsite becomes heavy clay mud after rain.

Riding the full length of the Central Road brings cyclists in contact with virtually every ecosystem found in the park. There are dense spruce stands, aspen groves, open grasslands, and old homesteads along the first portion of the trail. The road winds past marshes and beaver ponds, and cuts across creeks. About half way (43 km from the bison enclosure) you enter the beautiful Birdtail Valley, and then pass the bald Sugerloaf Hills, also known as the Birdtail Bench. Enjoy the view near the junction with the eastern leg of the Tilson Lake Trail. When riding east, enjoy the fast glide into the Birdtail Valley. For the most part, the Central Road is flat, level riding, with small rolling hills. The last 10 km hopscotch across hummocky hills to the Deep Lake Warden Station.

A description of the Central Road is also a listing of connecting trails and campsites. Trail connections which can be cycled and their distances west of the bison enclosure are: Grasshopper Valley Trail (2 km); Long Lake Road (9 km); Baldy Lake Road (31 km); and Sugarloaf Road (48 km). Campsites are located as follows: Minnedosa River (2 km); Whitewater Lake (11 km- site of a World War II prisoner of war camp); Gunn Lake (26 km- campsite is 2 km

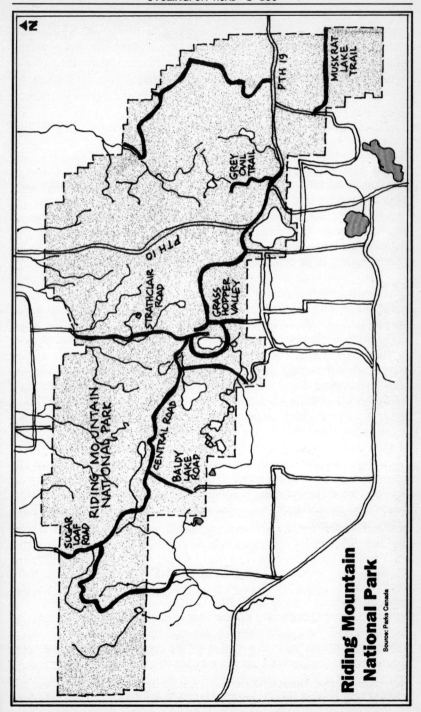

N

PTH 19

MUSKRAT LAKE TRAIL

GREY OWL TRAIL

PTH 10

STRATHCLAIR ROAD

GRASS HOPPER VALLEY

CENTRAL ROAD

BALDY LAKE ROAD

RIDING MOUNTAIN NATIONAL PARK

SUGAR LOAF ROAD

Riding Mountain National Park

Source: Parks Canada

along trail, but this is not a designated cycling route); Gunn Creek (39 km); Birdtail (50 km- campsite is 2 km southeast along the Tilson Lake Trail, but this is not a designated cycling route); and Deep Lake (70 km). Descriptions of the connecting trails are provided below. Check the maps, read the descriptions, then devise the mountain bike trek of your dreams.

Grasshopper Valley

Type: Off road day rides; trails and back roads.
Access: Loop beginning and ending in the Lake Audy Campground. Follow Lake Audy Road south to the Lake Audy Dam picnic site. Cross the dam and continue along the trail.
Facilities: Camping, picnic, latrines and water at Lake Audy Campground. Latrines and water at Minnedosa River primitive campground.
Distance: 18 km return.
Difficulty: Easy to moderate (easy distance and hills; moderate surface).

The Grasshopper Valley is as diminutive as its namesake insect. A rolling fescue prairie walled by aspen, it provides a pleasant day ride for families. For campers at Lake Audy it is a delightful spin, with no need to transport the bikes.

The first few kilometers past the Lake Audy picnic site afford good views of the lake as the trail skirts sedge wetlands. Follow the jog to the west, then swing north with the trail and follow the prairie of the Grasshopper Valley for 4 km. Swoop along the gentle hills of this section. The trail dives into a thick stand of spruce and aspen before arriving at the Minnedosa River. Negotiating this area can be the trickiest part of the ride if beavers have flooded the trail. Check with parks officials before heading out about the trail condition, or just take the chance and pit your ingenuity against that of the beavers.

Continue east past the primitive campsite, ignoring the turnoff to the north (left) which leads to the Central Trail (unless you want to connect with additional kilometers of riding). The trail bumps up against the fence of the bison enclosure. Follow it southward for 4 km of easy road riding back to Lake Audy Campground.

Long Lake Road

Type: Off road day rides or tours; back roads.
Access: Southern access and parking near Heron Creek Warden Station, north of PR 359. Park at the gated access road on the park boundary, and cycle a beautiful and traffic free road to the Warden Station. Northern access by bicycle from the Central Road, 9 km west of the bison enclosure.
Facilities: Water and latrines at Long Lake primitive campsite.
Distance: 14 km one way. Extended day trip or overnight tour of 54 km (29

km of trails, plus 25 km of gravel roads) possible in combination with
Grasshopper Valley Trail.
Difficulty: Easy to difficult (overall easy unless trail flooded by beaver
activity).

The Long Lake Road is a long road with sometimes too much lake. Beavers
have flooded the trail frequently over the last few years, especially just south
of Long Lake. Along the rest of the road the gravel surface allows fast, easy
spinning through mixed forests. The only destination, 10 km along the trail, is
Long Lake, reputed to have good pike fishing.

For fit cyclists, the Long Lake Road gains stature as part of a longer loop in
combination with the Grasshopper Valley Trail. Begin at either the Heron
Creek Warden Station or the Lake Audy Campground; for either route there
is an overnight campsite at approximately halfway. From Lake Audy travel
south on the main gravel road to the Lake Audy dam picnic site. Hook up with
the Grasshopper Valley Trail, taking the short spur near the Minnedosa River
campsite onto the Central Road. Follow this road to the west (left turn) for 6.5
km before turning south (left) onto the Long Lake Road. Keep churning the
pedals along the road, past the Heron Creek Warden Station. Continue on this
winding road among the lakes and the aspen. Turn east (left) at the junction
and follow the curves to the turnoff to the north (left) to Audy Lake. Note that
this road is not signposted: follow the municipal roads carefully on the detailed
trail map prepared by Parks Canada to identify the turn. A sign advertising the
Lake Audy Store may mark this junction, but don't count on it. Pass through
the poplars to the grassy meadows of Lake Audy. Check with Parks Canada
staff on the condition of Long Lake Road before setting out on this ride.

Baldy Lake Road

Type: Off road day rides with connections for tours; back roads.
Access: Southern access and parking at Baldy Lake Warden Station off PR
577. Turn north at the Marco cairn, then jog briefly east, then north (right,
then left) to reach the Warden Station. Northern access by bicycle from
Central Road, 31 km west of the bison enclosure, and 42 km east of Deep
Lake Warden Station.
Facilities: None.
Distance: 10 km one way. Several possibilities to connect to longer loops or
one way rides.
Difficulty: Easy to moderate (easy distance and surface; moderate hills).

A sweet little trail, Baldy Lake attracts all levels of cyclists. Its key appeal is the
excellent riding surface in a pleasing setting. The aspens snuggle cozily
around the trail, with glimpses of grasslands (watch for elk) and ponds (watch
or moose) on both sides. Situated in hummocky glacial deposits, the road rolls

gently, with the occasional long hill. Near the southern end of the road, a short trail leads to Baldy Lake.

By itself the trail has no definite destination, but with an additional 4.5 km along the Central Road the trailhead to Gunn Lake is reached. The Gunn Lake Trail is not a designated bicycle route, but it is only a 2 km walk to the water and the campsite.

Include the Baldy Lake Road in a longer tour along the Central Road. One suggestion is to follow the Central Road via Gunn Creek campsite (20 km) to the western end of the park, with pick-up at Deep Lake Campground (51 km from start). Ride a full circle tour by cruising the gravel roads of the Birdtail Valley from Deep Lake back to the Baldy Lake Warden Station (p.103; 90 km total). Consider another tour, describing a full or partial loop via the Long Lake Road (p.160; 95 km total).

Sugarloaf Road

Type: Off road day rides with connections for tours; back roads.
Access: Northern access and parking at Sugarloaf Warden Station. Southern access by bicycle from Central Road, 48 km west of the bison enclosure, and 25 km east of Deep Lake Warden Station.
Facilities: None.
Distance: 8 km one way. Trailhead to Gunn Creek Campsite on Central Road 19 km one way; Deep Lake Campground to trailhead 22 km one way.
Difficulty: Easy to moderate (easy distance and surface; moderate hills).

It is a shame that the excellent views from the Sugarloaf Road are not seen and appreciated by more cyclists, but the relative inaccessibility of the trailhead is a deterrent. The best views of the Sugarloaf Hills themselves are from the Central Road, just 1 km south of the southern end of the Sugarloaf Road. Here, the bald Sugarloaf Hills complement the scenic creases of the Birdtail Valley.

From the trailhead warden station south, aspens quake on both sides of the trail. Pass the wetlands and the recent construction initiatives of beavers. Soon the high rolling hills begin. Swoop from crest to valley, stopping to admire the view. All too soon the trail descends gracefully into the valley, and the junction with the Central Road is met.

Include the Sugarloaf Road in a mountain bike tour along Central Road. Spend a day and ride unencumbered from the Gunn Creek campsite (38 km return). Strong cyclists could explore this hilly route from the Deep Lake Campground in one day (44 km return).

Roaring River Canyon

The Roaring River Canyon is as wonderful as its name. While the 'canyon' label on the topographic map seems extreme, this secret part of Manitoba boasts a steep walled valley, superb scenery, and a river that really does roar in spring. The Roaring River Canyon is located in the northern portion of Duck Mountain Provincial Forest. The trail starts at the edge of the Swan River Valley and climbs up onto the Manitoba Escarpment, where the Roaring River carved its valley into the escarpment slope. Many of the trails in the canyon are said to be ancient Indian paths. Follow them through mature balsam poplar and spruce forests, across patches of prairie, and up and down the constant hills.

It all makes for good mountain biking, especially if exploratory riding and tough terrain appeal to you. There is not an extensive network of trails, but an out-and-back day ride is very satisfying. Cycling the Roaring River Canyon is backcountry riding, so be prepared and carry snacks, water, tools and maps, and pay attention to navigation. Topographic map 62 N/14 may be useful in identifying landscape features, but the trail described below is not on it. In spring be prepared for wet riding, and watch for she-bears with young. This is among the finest of Manitoba mountain biking: a fascinating area, challenging riding, and a sense of exploration and history.

Type: Off road day rides and tours; trails.
Access: Take the first grid road west of the junction of PR 486 and PR 488 in the Swan River Valley, and travel south to the end of the road. The road ends and the trail begins on private property. Ask permission to park, and to cross Ron Galbraith's land.
Facilities: None at trailhead. Primitive campsites along trail with no facilities. Nearest full facilities in Swan River.
Distance: Trail length described is approximately 8 km one way. Longer rides possible.
Difficulty: Moderate to difficult (distances, hills and surface).

Access to the trail is from the field behind Ron Galbraith's house. At about halfway along the field, take the trail leading steeply up the hill. After the initial climb, it joins the main trail running into the valley. Turn south (right). This trail is wide and generally well kept, but there may be a lot of dead fall to hop or scramble over. Zoom and pant down and up the constant hills, fording the frequent streams at the bottom. In a wet spring, numerous wet spots and muddy sections lurk around corners, but there are also many kilometers of delightful riding. The trail parallels the valley, enclosed within a mature

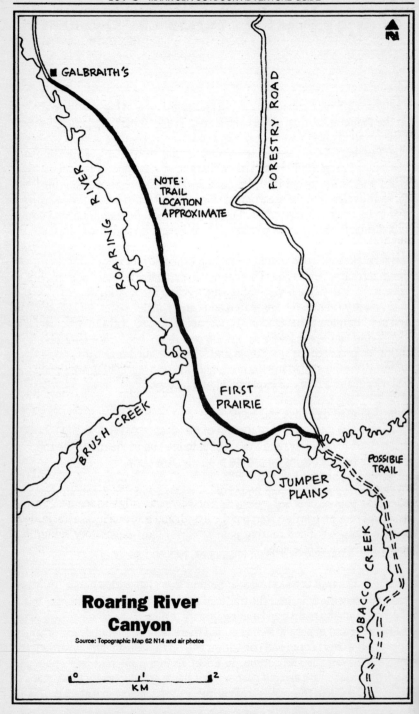

GALBRAITH'S

FORESTRY ROAD

ROARING RIVER

NOTE:
TRAIL
LOCATION
APPROXIMATE

FIRST
PRAIRIE

BRUSH CREEK

JUMPER
PLAINS

POSSIBLE
TRAIL

TOBACCO CREEK

**Roaring River
Canyon**

Source: Topographic Map 62 N14 and air photos

0   1   2
KM

deciduous forest, and initially the view is limited to glimpses and hints.

Occasionally small trails branch off from the main trail. Ignore these for the most part. However, turn to the southwest (right) at the first major branch in this direction. This junction occurs in the middle of a long wet section in the trail, and the branch clearly goes up a hill. The turn has been marked with red flagging tape, but don't count on this. If you miss this turn, you'll soon know it: the trail which continues straight eventually peters out, becoming heavily overgrown with shrubs. A further check on this turn is the location of a small, recently logged ravine: if you can glimpse this ravine to your left, you've made the turn correctly; if you can see it clearly to your right, then retrace your steps.

After making the correct turn, climb to the top of the hill, then descend. Ignore the next junction to the right and continue straight, crossing a stream along the way, into stands of conifers. Suddenly the trail opens out into a clearing at the side of the Roaring River. Rest, swim or camp here. The valley walls are not steep but the force of the river is apparent from its twisted course and eroded banks.

The trail re-enters dense forest and begins to climb slowly upward. The trail dramatically emerges onto an open grassland, marked on the topographical map as 'First Prairie'. Watch for elk, which venture from the protection of the forest to graze on the grasses. Although the grassland can resist invasion by trees, the prairie ecosystem is vulnerable to human disturbance, demonstrated by the persistence of several trails across this prairie. Follow the most obvious one, which curves slightly up and to the left.

Now the trail climbs through big aspen trees, occasionally dipping, but progressively climbing the hillside. At the highest part, the reward is a viewpoint perched on a precipitous cliff. Survey the close, steep walls of the Roaring River Canyon, and look across the valley to another prairie called 'Jumper Plains'. Although not visible, the river rushes audibly below. From the viewpoint, zip steeply downhill to the intersection with a logging road (marked on the topographic map).

Return to the start by backtracking along the same route, or try the logging road back to Swan River Valley, returning to your car via municipal roads. The latter has not been checked by bicycle, but it is apparently less scenic. The trail also continues across the river, but the length and trail quality are not known. Longer trails may open touring possibilities. Enjoy exploratory riding in a beautiful region of Manitoba.

Sandilands Provincial Forest

A long, wide band of green, Sandilands Provincial Forest dominates off road riding in southeastern Manitoba. Layers of sand were deposited during the glacial period, with hills another glacial legacy, especially along the western edge of the forest. Hills and forests combine for wonderful mountain biking in parts of Sandilands, while in other areas extensive sand eliminates any pleasure. Select rides from the two cross country ski trail systems and from the network of forestry roads.

All levels of cyclists can enjoy Sandilands. Long distance kilometers entice racers, while short loops and beautiful scenery suit recreational cyclists. Spring is an especially beautiful time to cycle in Sandilands. The sandy trails are ridable soon after the snow melts, and prairie crocuses burst open on the hillsides. When other areas are too wet in summer or fall, try Sandilands. As with other parts of southeastern Manitoba, biting flies are aggressive in summer.

Sandilands Ski Trail

Type: Off road day rides; trails and back roads.
Access: Two good access points to the trails: wayside park on PR 210 east of Marchand and just past junction with PR 404; or first roadside parking area at crest of hill on PR 404 south of PR 210. Look for large wooden trail map.
Facilities: Picnic tables, latrines and water at wayside park on PR 210. No other facilities on trail. Nearest full facilities at Marchand.
Distance: Total trail distance of 52 km, with individual trails as follows:

Red Trail (one way)	5 km
Green Trail	13 km
Yellow Trail	9 km
Blue Trail	10 km

Difficulty: Easy to moderate (distances, hills and surface).

The southern cross country ski trails in Sandilands Provincial Forest offer many kilometers of wonderful riding. When the snow melts, a whole new system of ATC trails also appears for exploration. The scenery in Sandilands is one of the pleasures of riding there. Jack pine proliferates in every conceiv-

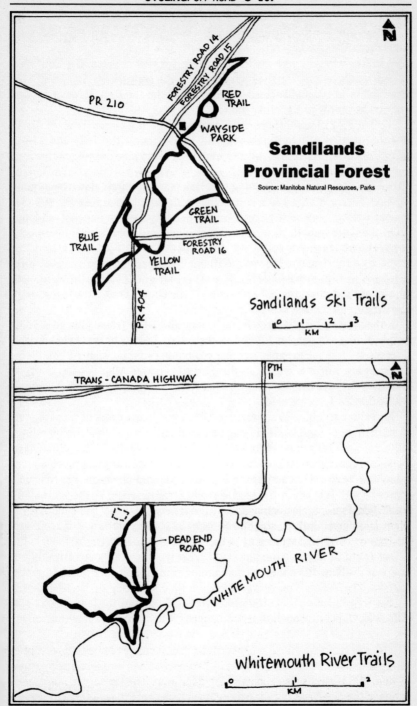

Sandilands Ski Trails

Whitemouth River Trails

able shape. Periodically birch and aspen intrude with dazzling white stands, and there is even the rare red pine. Look for prairie flowers and grasses underneath the trees.

From the wayside park on PR 210 there are two choices: the Red Trail leading north, or crossing the highway to join the network of other trails. The Red Trail is an out-and-back trail, and rates as the sandiest. It is not recommended as highly as the other trails.

South of PR 210, a short spur trail connects with the Green Trail. At the T-junction, turn south (left). Swoop and twist around the hills and turns, galloping through jack pine and a special stand of red pine to another junction. Turn west (right) onto the level wide road; turning left will take you back to PR 210. Skim along this road, flashing past jack pine and birch, down to another junction. Straight ahead is a connection with the trails across PR 404, described below. Turn to the north (right) to complete the Green Trail loop. Scoot along the smooth surface, crossing several wide roads but ignoring any turns. The trail begins to roll gently, then dips down to a T-junction among the pines. It's a short spin to the west (left) out to the parking area on PR 404. To return to the wayside park on PR 210, turn north (right), climb to the viewpoint, then zip up and down the hilliest section of the Green Trail, back to the short spur leading to the wayside park.

To the west of PR 404 stretch the Yellow and Blue Trails, plus an infinite variety of miscellaneous roads and tracks. Learn the area by first following the ski trails, then set off to explore as many kilometers as you wish. Although the ski trails are not marked on it, the Forestry Tower Map Section 5 (from Manitoba Surveys and Mapping), rather than the topographic map, provides orientation for forestry roads.

The Yellow and Blue Trails excel in hills. They loop up and down along the western ridge of Sandilands, mixing beautiful scenery and challenging riding. If the trail isn't hilly enough for you, grind up some of the hills leading off to the side. From the junction of the Green and Yellow Trails described above, follow the Yellow Trail across the forestry road and down the big hills and across PR 404. Just before the road is another trail junction. To the south (left) is the Blue Trail, to the north (right) is the shorter return of the Yellow Trail.

The Blue Trail skirts the bottom of rocky hills, then vaults over a few. After the trail veers north it crosses a road. Cruise this road east (right) back to PR 404, or continue north on the Blue Trail. Nearby, the return loop of the Yellow Trail has thrilling downhills and demanding climbs. Enjoy the views from the hill tops. The Yellow Trail merges with the Blue, and they zip together along the base of a hillside of dazzling white birches. Negotiate the few wet sections of the trail, then grunt up the final hill back to PR 404. Cross the road, and rejoin the Green Trail for the fast ride back to the wayside park.

The Whitemouth River Trails

Type: Off road day rides; trails and back roads.
Access: Most easily reached west of the end of PTH 11, south of the Trans-Canada Highway. Follow the curve of the road to the west, and go past the forestry center. The trails are unmarked in summer, but lead from the first road to the south after the forestry center: look for trails into the forest on both sides of the road. Park along the main road.
Facilities: None at trailhead or along trail. Nearest facilities at Hadashville.
Distance: Total trail length approximately 10 km, with individual loops between 2.5 km and 7 km.
Difficulty: Easy (distances, hills and surface).

This little trail system tucked beside the Whitemouth River offers great scenery and a beautiful riding surface. Beginning in dense jack pine, the trail loops across grassy meadows, into riverbank forest, and past an island of black spruce forest. The hills are low and the riding is easy. The Whitemouth River trails are ideal for families and recreational cyclists. The sandy base allows riding even in wet weather, and when it's dry there are only a few patches of deep sand to bypass.

From the main road, select the trail leading to the west, furthest away from the forestry center. Cruise along the mat of pine needles, past a fence, and turn southeast (left) at the first junction. After more jack pines and easy spinning, there is a second junction with a broader road. Turn east (left) and follow it past the dead-end road. There are two choices: a trail straight ahead, or one that swoops down a small hill to the south (right). Choose the latter, taking the turn to the west (right) at the bottom. Flit across this grassy area, taking the next turn to the south (left) onto the winding riverbank trail among the poplars. Take time to look for muskrats and beaver along the river. Near the end of this trail an unusual ridge sheers briefly upward.

Several trails intersect just west of the ridge. Facing west with the ridge behind you, the first trail to the north (right) swings back to the start of the riverbank trail. Ahead, two trails diverge in jack pines and sand. The road to the left, not a ski trail, meanders further south with the river, inviting exploration. Follow the ski trail to the west (right; marked with orange signs) which circles above and around a dense knot of black spruce. At the next junction a trail leads north (right), past the fence to the starting point. An alternate return is to continue straight, briefly retracing your tire tracks to the dead-end road. This time go straight into the jack pines, veering north (left) at the first junction. Twist, turn and roll through the thick trees back to the main road.

This route has introduced you to most of the designated ski trails at the Whitemouth River. Gain a little familiarity with these trails, then set off to explore some of the intersecting roads used by trail bikes, or the nearby network of forestry roads.

The Forestry Roads

An extensive network of roads cuts through all corners of Sandilands Provincial Forest, especially just south of the Trans-Canada Highway. The Forestry Tower Map Section 5 illustrates all these numbered roads. Navigation is easy with this map, as most of the road junctions are signposted. Some of the roads also have historical interest: PR 505 and Road #29 are part of the old Dawson Trail used by settlers, while Road #31 was a former provincial boundary.

Virtually any combination of roads, including many circle routes, could be ridden in Sandilands. Ride from either of the two trail systems described above, or use the hamlets of Sandilands, Woodridge or Richer as a base. Via PR 506 connect with Agassiz Provincial Forest (p.115).

Riding the roads of Sandilands is not as enjoyable as exploring the Sandilands trails or the Agassiz back roads. Many of the roads in Sandilands Provincial Forest are very sandy and the northern area is flat, with seemingly endless jack pines, spruces and aspens. Some of the roads are also very rough, with a jolting 'washboard' surface. Come to the forestry roads of Sandilands when you're in the mood for long-distance solitude, or when your exploratory sense is strong.

Snow Valley and Birch

Tucked into the folds of the Pembina Hills, Snow Valley stands as a special part of Manitoba. The hills and valleys which have historically separated the valley from the adjacent Red River plains today provide sensational mountain biking. The joys of the gravel road network are many (p.99), and for the adventurous, the off road pleasures are even greater. This is the training ground of many racers, offering demanding hills and technical challenges. The focus of the trails are two downhill and cross country ski areas near Roseisle: Snow Valley and Birch. Grind up the ski hills, scoot along the cross country trails, creep down cow paths, or skim the occasional back road. These trails are not suited to beginners or families: they are too long and arduous.

Some starting suggestions are provided below. Head out on your own, or find someone familiar with the area for your first ride. Snow Valley saw its first mountain bike race in 1988, and more are planned; racing or touring the course is a good way to learn the trails. The land around Snow Valley and Birch is all private. Please ask permission at the ski resorts before heading out, and respect the land and property. Remember that you ride at your own risk. Topographic map 62 G/8 identifies major landforms, but the trails are not shown. The Manitoba Orienteering Association has produced a map of the area. Riding at Snow Valley and Birch is wonderful in all seasons, although some areas are muddy after rain.

Type: Off road day rides; trails.
Access: Start from either Snow Valley or Birch Ski Resorts. Both are off PR 245, just west of Roseisle. To reach Snow Valley Ski Resort, continue straight west from the main street of Roseisle, around the curves, up the hill and down to the foot of Snow Valley resort. Birch is reached by turning south at the first municipal road west of Roseisle. Take the next turn to the west (right) and climb the hill in two stages to the top of the ski area.
Facilities: None at trailheads or along trails. Store in Roseisle; nearest full facilities in Carman.
Distance: Undefined. Rides of virtually any length can be selected.
Difficulty: Difficult (moderate distances and surfaces; difficult hills).

From the bottom of the Snow Valley Ski Resort there are two ways of getting to the trails at the top of the ski hills. Straight up is the fastest and most anaerobic route. The slopes to the south (right as you face the hill) are slightly more forgiving. Follow the general curve of this right-hand hill to the left, ignoring the trail straight ahead, towards a T-junction near the top. Up and to the left takes you to the very top of the downhill slopes and a good view; up and

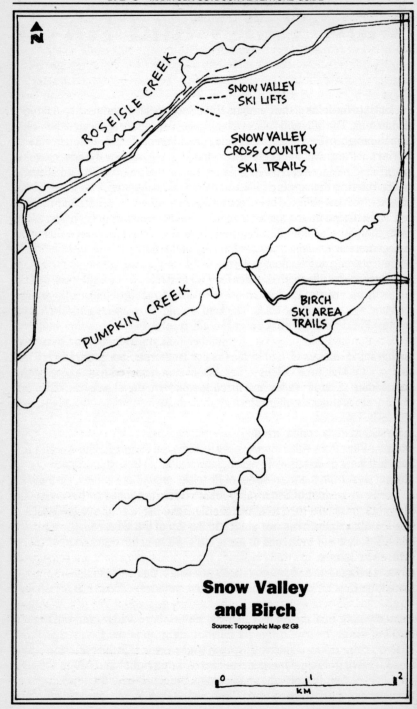

N

SNOW VALLEY
SKI LIFTS

ROSEISLE CREEK

SNOW VALLEY
CROSS COUNTRY
SKI TRAILS

PUMPKIN CREEK

BIRCH
SKI AREA
TRAILS

Snow Valley
and Birch

Source: Topographic Map 62 G8

0   1   2
KM

to the right brings you to an oak-lined ridge.

A longer but more gradual climb is to backtrack east from the property gates along the gravel road towards Roseisle. At the crest of the hill, a path to the south (right) leads into the cross country trails. Keep to the south (right) at the first junction and the trail leads to the halfway point on the downhill slopes. A demanding climb to the top rewards with a view and access to the cross country trails. From the view point climb past the lift equipment to the top of another hill. To the east is a trail which zips down then straight up another hill. Take this route to the trails and the oak-lined ridge.

The trails are only signposted in the winter, and there is a confusing welter of them. The following are rough directions to the Pumpkin Creek valley and to the Birch Ski area, which is essentially south and east of the Snow Valley Resort. From the oak-tree lined ridge, take the following turns at each junction: left; right to travel along the edge of a field; left at the bottom of the field, then immediately right; up a hill, turning left to follow the edge of another field; right onto a dirt track beside an electric fence; left at the top of the hill, and briefly follow the field to an immediate left over an electric fence; right just before the trail goes back up a hill. After descending this last hill, you will find that the forest opens up into a pasture, with Pumpkin Creek in the bottom of the valley. Look across to the hills of Birch. Once you know this area, you will discover at least half a dozen ways to reach the same point.

To return to Snow Valley ride across the cow pasture to where a distinct cow path leads up to the northwest into the oak trees near an electric fence. Twist and turn through the trees, emerging into the open, and veering up another hill to the left. At the top is a field enclosed by a fence. Follow this to the north (left turn), climbing up the trail at the end of the open area. Follow the top, scream down the hill, and turn to the right, nipping under the electric fence. Climb this hill and at the top, turn north (left) onto the road. Swoop up and down, past the electric fence to the left, hanging a sharp right, and you are back onto the route which you came up. Explore alternate routes back, selecting those that lead down.

On the opposite hillside from the cow pasture in Pumpkin Creek are the downhill runs of the Birch Ski Area. Ford the creek (no set location) and climb the ski hills to gain access to the Birch cross country trails. From the top of the ski hill, follow the wide road to the north (left) to reach the Birch ski lodge. The cross country ski trails at Birch are enclosed in a much more compact area, starting from and looping back to the ski lodge. An intricate network of parallel and connecting trails is set on the steep hillside. Directions are difficult to give, as trails wrap around each other and are unmarked. Set off and explore, remembering that the trails loop back to the lodge, which is on the highest point of land.

Even more riding is possible by combining these ski trails with the gravel roads (p.99), the abandoned rail line and other trails into the hidden recesses of this area. Respect private property; ask permission before crossing, then enjoy some of the prettiest and hilliest mountain biking in Manitoba.

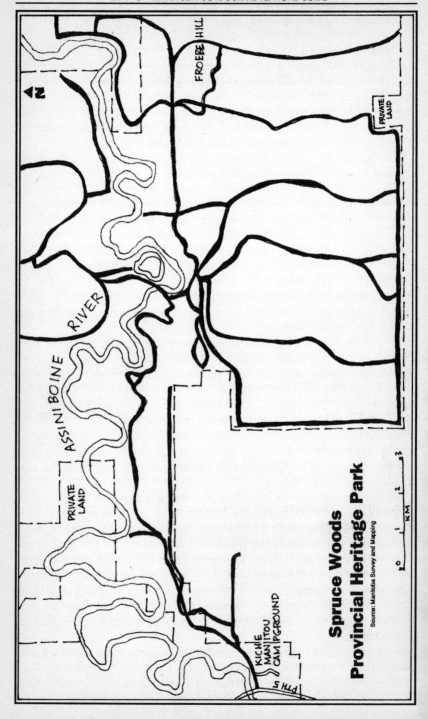

Spruce Woods
Provincial Heritage Park

Source: Manitoba Survey and Mapping

Spruce Woods Provincial Heritage Park

Spruce Woods Provincial Heritage Park stands out as a fascinating and unique corner of Manitoba, and the mountain biking possibilities here exude a similar charm. The park encompasses the Spirit Sands Hills, active sand dunes reminiscent of arid climates, as well as a blend of prairie, forest and riverine ecosystems. The sand dunes are excluded from mountain biking, both to protect the fragile environment and to save cyclists' sanity from the extensive sand. Nonetheless, hundreds of scenic kilometers beckon, showing off the amazing variety and beauty of the park.

There are two main mountain biking areas: the snowmobile and vehicle route trails south of the Assiniboine River, and the cross country ski trail systems diverging from PTH 5 further north. One trail in each of these areas is described in detail, along with suggestions for other rides. Spruce Woods is best suited to experienced cyclists who will enjoy the variety and challenges of the park, including steep hills and patches of sand. Ride Spruce Woods in all the cycling seasons. It's a good choice after rain, although the trails may become muddy in the river valley.

South of the Assiniboine River

Type: Off road day rides; back roads and trails.
Access: Southern trails accessed off PTH 5, on the road to Kiche Manitou Campgrounds. There is a parking area at the western end of the trails but it is not obvious in the summer. A better access is to follow the gravel road (keeping left) to the dead end.
Facilities: None at trailhead or along trails. Camping, stores, water and washrooms at campground. Nearest full facilities in Carberry or Glenboro.
Distance: Variable, depending on trails used. Options for very long rides.
Difficulty: Easy to moderate (distance, hills and surface).

A series of snowmobile trails, hunting roads and other tracks provide an extensive network of trails south of the river and east of PTH 5. In many cases the snowmobile tracks overlap or parallel hunting roads. Navigation is difficult south of the Assiniboine because the snowmobile trails are not clearly marked in summer, and there are many interconnecting trails. Topographic map 62 G/ 11 provides general orientation, but trails are not marked. Manitoba Department of Natural Resources produces a very useful Plan of Vehicle Routes in Spruce Woods Provincial Park. Explore these trails when you are prepared to wander a little, satisfied with just knowing your general location. Be prepared for some hills and sandy tracks at times, but also lots of enjoyment.

At the dead end of the gravel road lies the greatest choice of trails, especially loops. There are two basic directions to select: west or southeast. Two snowmobile trails run virtually parallel to the west, with the most obvious one starting as a sandy road leading to the northwest (extreme left, facing the dead end). Bounce and jolt over the first few km, grinding across prairie and through recently cleared areas with low shrub stumps. The trail is especially difficult to follow here, but keep heading basically west. Negotiate the deep ruts carved by four-wheel drive vehicles. Several farm roads intersect, but these generally lead to riverbank fields on private land. Respect the fences marking the park's boundary. Perseverance is ultimately rewarded with smoother riding and several excellent views overlooking the Assiniboine River Valley. The trails cross or come close to the main dirt road several times. Return to the start at any of these points along the road, or follow the snowmobile trail to the bottom of the loop near the campground. To return from the end of the loop, follow the road briefly to the northeast (right), watching for the turnoff of the return trail into the bush to the north (left). Work your way back, essentially parallel to your route out.

Choose from among the many trails in the southeast corner of the park. The snowmobile tracks often parallel old roads which offer easier riding, despite many sandy patches. One loop which passes through virtually every type of ecosystem found in Spruce Woods Park swings in a circle to the east of the dead end. Leaving the end of the road, follow the car tracks down the hill to the south (right). Keep to the left for the first three junctions. Initially the trail passes through short grass prairie sprinkled with blue grama grass and sage. After the first junction the trail enters mixed spruce and deciduous forest. After descending a long hill into a remnant riverbank elm forest, the track passes through a farmer's field and leads to an oxbow lake graced by an old log cabin. Turn north (right) at the lake, then west (left) at the next junction. Get up some speed and crank hard through the bulrushes and sedges, which are passable even in spring. The road then winds along the river, traversing more fields and pastures before gradually rising into an open coniferous forest to intersect the main dirt road. Turn east (left) onto the road to return to the dead end.

Long kilometers of trails run north to south in seven parallel lines in the southeast corner. They are connected along the southern boundary and at the northern extremity, near the river. These trails have not been checked by bicycle, but they are apparently enclosed entirely in spruce and aspen forests, crossing only mildly undulating land. Consider searching for oxbow lakes or Froeboe Hill in the southeast area of the park.

Northwestern Trails

Type: Off road day rides and tours; trails and back roads.

Access: The Epinette Creek Trails have the most northern access from PTH 5. Watch for the trail signs along the same road as several camps. Take the fork to the east (right) to reach the trail head. The turnoff for the Seton Trails is less than one kilometer further south on PTH 5; the parking area and trail head is immediately west of the highway. The Yellow Quill Trails are 3 km further south, around the bend of PTH 5: the access road is not marked.

Facilities: Huts, latrines and water at the Epinette Creek trailhead and at several points along these trails. Nearest full facilities in Carberry or Glenboro.

Distance: Several trails in the three systems as follows:

Epinette Creek Trail system

Spruce Trail	2.0 km
Juniper Trail	1.5 km
Tamarack Trail	
-north	5.0 km
-south	4.5 km
Newfoundland Trail	24.4 km
Seton Trail system	18.2 km
Yellow Quill Trail system	13 km

Difficulty: Moderate to difficult (moderate to difficult distances and hills; easy to moderate surface).

Three cross country ski and hiking trails open up more delightful riding in Spruce Woods Provincial Heritage Park. The most extensive and the most recommended system is that centered around Epinette Creek. The Epinette Creek and Newfoundland Trails crisscross the diversity of ecosystems which characterize Spruce Woods. The trails wind with the creek bends, scoot up and down valley walls, cavort across grasslands, and dance between spruce and aspen. Several campsites open the trails to overnight touring, in addition to day ride pleasures. Campers should obtain backcountry camping permits at the Spruce Woods Visitor Centre. Note that the cabins along the trail are for winter or emergency use only.

From the parking area the trail snuggles against the creek, then branches into two trails on each bank which converge, before the trail balloons into the wide, long circle of the Newfoundland Trail. The route is signed in summer as a hiking trail and directions are clear. This hiking and cycling trail has been recently re-routed from the original cross country ski trail, so that hikers and cyclists can linger longer in the river valley. Watch for stumps and roughness along the new trail sections, although this will improve with time. Watch for hikers, especially when zipping around corners or zooming downhill.

Hop up onto the hill to the north (left) of the hut at the parking area to begin cycling the Epinette Creek Trails. Wander through the spruce and aspen,

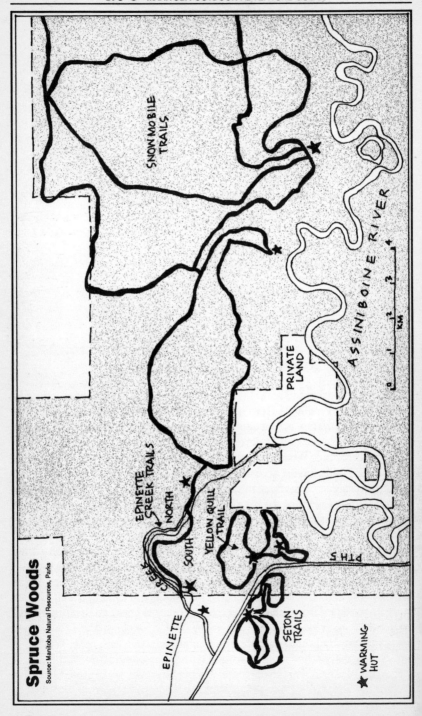

Spruce Woods

Source: Manitoba Natural Resources, Parks

SNOW MOBILE TRAILS

ASSINIBOINE RIVER

PRIVATE LAND

KM

EPINETTE CREEK TRAILS

NORTH

SOUTH

YELLOW QUILL TRAIL

CREEK

EPINETTE

PTHS

SETON TRAILS

★ WARMING HUT

crossing the creek twice, and freewheeling and climbing in and out of the valley. The trail soon leaves private pasture, crossing a turnstile fence into the park. Pedal on through the aspens to the first campsite, nestled at the bottom of a hill. Ride up the hill onto the prairie, veering with the trail markers to the northeast.

The trail races across the prairie and skips through spruce and aspen before plunging into the river valley. This is the basic pattern for the rest of the ride. The trail dips in and out of the river valley with demanding ascents and screaming descents. Walk your bike down (and up) some of the steeper valley walls. The rewards are sensational views. Gaze across grasslands with islands of spruces, and peer into the wooded creek valley before teetering over the edge.

Approximately halfway along the trail the first junction confronts you. Here the trail branches into routes along the north bank (left) and along the south bank (right). While both offer hills and views, the south bank is slightly less arduous than the north bank. The two trails converge just before the third camping area, which is beautifully situated overlooking the ravine of the creek. If the third cabin is your destination, return by backtracking briefly, then choosing the north or south bank routes (south to the left; north to the right). Pedal, pant, and push up the hills, and thrill to some sensational downhills. After the convergence of the trails, retrace your route back to the parking area, cycling past the second campsite, clambering across the turnstile gate, and recrossing the creek twice.

From the third cabin, a short spur with very steep hills leads to the two halves of the Newfoundland Trail. Although it sees less use than the other trails, the riding surface remains good. In a day trip, ride either the North Route or the South Route as far as desired before turning back. Head for the fourth campsite at Jackfish Lake for an overnight tour. Directions are easy along these routes since there are no turns required. Several old roads intersect the trail but junctions are marked. The North Route specializes in prairie mixed with spruce and aspen, while the south loop is slightly more wooded.

Explore additional kilometers of cycling on the Seton and Yellow Quill Trail systems. Check with Parks on the availability of the Seton trails, which are located outside the park on crown land: in some years they may be fenced and used as cattle pasture. Neither the Seton nor the Yellow Quill Trails have been checked by bicycle, but the terrain is very similar to that found along the Epinette Creek Trail system: hilly with patches of forest amid grasslands dotted with solitary spruces. Yellow Quill sports more rolling prairie, while Seton tends to sand, and has steeper hills. Watch your turns and directions, particularly in the Seton system, as several trails radiate from the two cabins. The Yellow Quill Trails are dissected by an old road which continues further west across private land to reach the Epinette Creek trail head.

Other Rides

Further snowmobile trails and Designated Vehicle Routes wind through the northeastern section of the park. This area offers tremendous potential for exploratory mountain bikers. Although access is not clear, it may be possible to connect with these trails from roads intersecting the Newfoundland Trail. The map produced by Manitoba Department of Natural Resources, titled Plan of Vehicle Routes in Spruce Woods Provincial Park, is the best source of inspiration.

One area of Spruce Woods Provincial Heritage Park is definitely taboo for mountain biking: the Spirit Sands Trail. Enjoy the sand dunes from the walking trails, and head further east to the network of ridable trails, north and south of the Assiniboine River.

The Spruce Woods trails can be combined with a variety of gravel or paved road adventures, including the Mouse and Turtle Tour (p.36), the Lavenham Area (p.85) and the Treesbank Circuit (p.105).

Turtle Mountain Provincial Park

Turtle Mountain Provincial Park offers the closest thing to paradise in Manitoba when it comes to fast, easy-spinning, mountain biking. The joys of this southwestern park are numerous. Over 150 km of roads and trails crisscross the park, all with a consistently smooth surface. A different lake seems to pop up around each curve, and over every hill there is a new chance to startle a white-tailed deer or glimpse a goshawk or grouse.

Cyclists of all ages and abilities can revel in Turtle Mountain. The trails are ideal for beginners looking for a manageable challenge: here you can ride hills in the backwoods without terrifying downhills or difficult ascents. Navigation is easy along the well-marked trails. More advanced cyclists can cover a lot of kilometers and climb a lot of hills. Add further variety and distance by cycling the gravel roads in the immediate vicinity of the park. Inject some backwoods cruising into the paved road Mouse and Turtle Tour (p.36).

There are two main off road riding areas in Turtle Mountain. A vast system of long distance gravel roads and trails covers the western two-thirds of the park. To the east lies an intricate network of shorter trails radiating from Adam Lake. One main trail in each section is described in detail, and an overview of the others is provided to whet your appetite for exploration. Turtle Mountain is wonderful whenever your inclination takes you there, but it is especially beautiful in autumn. Watch for slick mud on some of the trails after rain.

Western Roads and Trails

Type: Off road day rides; back roads and trails.
Access: The western trails of Turtle Mountain Provincial Park are accessed via PR 446 at Max Lake, or at the intersection of the West Main Road with PR 450, 14 km south of PTH 3. Best parking area and clearest trail access at Max Lake Campground. Western trails accessible by bicycle from the Adam Lake trails via the Boundary Road Trail.
Facilities: Camping and picnic facilities, latrines and drinking water at Max Lake. Nearest full facilities at Boissevain and at Metigoshe Lake (except indoor accommodation at the latter).
Distance: Various distances from a few to more than 100 km, along the following trails:
Bella Lake Trail   30 km

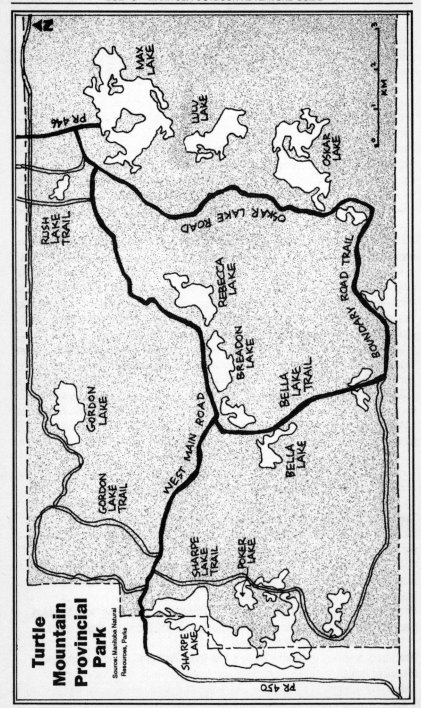

Turtle
Mountain
Provincial
Park

Source: Manitoba Natural
Resources, Parks

MAX LAKE

WILLY LAKE

OSKAR LAKE

PR 446

RUSH LAKE TRAIL

OSKAR LAKE ROAD

REBECCA LAKE

BREADON LAKE

BOUNDARY ROAD TRAIL

BELLA LAKE TRAIL

GORDON LAKE

WEST MAIN ROAD

BELLA LAKE

GORDON LAKE TRAIL

SHARPE LAKE TRAIL

POKER LAKE

SHARPE LAKE

PR 450

KM

N

Sharpe Lake Trail	43 km
Rush Lake Trail	8 km
Gordon Lake Trail	32 km

Difficulty: Moderate (moderate to difficult distances; moderate hills; easy surfaces).

Many kilometers of fun stretch out in the western section of the park. The rides are along winter snowmobile trails which vary from a high quality gravel road across the center of the park to excellent grassy trails. A particularly delightful loop along the Bella Lake Trail beckons from the Max Lake Campground. Strong riders could cycle this in less than two hours, but it can also be a pleasant day outing at a slower pace. Cycling counterclockwise leaves the easiest portion of the ride to the end.

From Max Lake Campground follow either the main road or the trail through the trees to the road which leads south to Oskar Lake. Eat up the kilometers easily on this wide, gravel surface. The hills begin rolling right away, carrying you past a succession of tiny lakes flashing blue through the aspens. Past the last of several active oil wells, the gravel disappears and the road narrows. This is the hilliest portion of the ride, but it's easy to scoot downhill, then zip up the next rise.

Turn west (right) at the clearly marked junction with the Boundary Road Trail. The trail narrows further, at times reduced to two ruts, but the pedaling remains easy. Skirt several larger lakes teeming with ducks. Manitoba maple, bur oak, green ash, trembling aspen, and beaked hazelnut proliferate along the Boundary Road Trail.

Leave the gentle rises of the Boundary Road Trail after approximately 4 km, to ride north (right) on the Bella Lake Trail. The riding surface changes markedly to a broad grassy path, but it remains surprisingly good. Unexpected holes or logs are rare. This is the wettest section of the route. Soon after starting north, the trail dips between two lakes and traverses a marshy area. It is easily crossed in a dry year, and at worst could give you a wet foot or two.

Stop at Bella Lake for a picnic or press on to the next junction, distinguished by a white spruce plantation. Turn east (right) at this junction onto the West Main Road, a broad, high quality road traveled infrequently by cars and trucks. The ascents and descents tend to be longer and more gradual, and it is a pleasurable spin for the final 9 km back to the starting point.

The Sharpe Lake Trail is the other major route best suited for off road riding in western Turtle Mountain Provincial Park. It bulges across the southwestern segment of the park. It can be reached in a long ride from Max Lake via the West Main Road or the Oskar Lake Road and Boundary Road Trail, or can be accessed from the west via PR 450, making a loop with the Bella Lake Trail.

The riding is generally easy, with most of the distance covered by a broad gravel road. At the western edge of the park the Sharpe Lake Trail zigzags south among numerous lakes, including two tips of Sharpe Lake. Near Poker Lake a road leads to the west (right) to a Boy Scout camp. Pass another trail

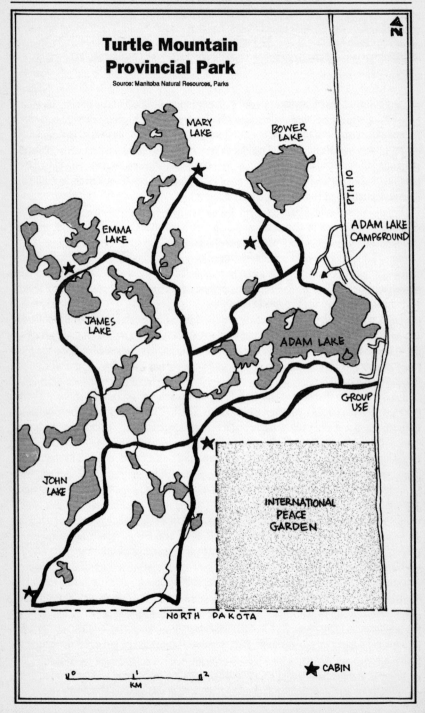

Turtle Mountain Provincial Park

Source: Manitoba Natural Resources, Parks

access, keeping to the east (left). The Sharpe Lake Trail acquires more of a trail quality as it runs southeast to meet the Boundary Road Trail. This section sports fewer hills and lakes, but is distinguished by extensive spruce plantations. Follow the Boundary Road Trail to the Bella Lake Trail. Choose to return either north along the Bella Lake Trail, or further east via the Oskar Lake Road.

The Gordon Lake Trail runs for 32 km across the northern third of Turtle Mountain Provincial Park, connecting with the northern end of the Sharpe Lake Trail. The Rush Lake Trail describes a short square near Max Lake. Both the Gordon Lake and Rush Lake Trails are connected by a long trail delineating much of the northern park boundary. These are trails rather than roads, and the surface may be rougher with occasional deadfall. Although these have not been checked by bicycle, they add more kilometers of enjoyment to one of the best and most extensive trail networks in Manitoba.

Eastern Trails

Type: Off road day rides or overnight tours; trails.
Access: The trails are accessed from the Adam Lake Campground on PTH 10. Follow the main road into the campground, turning west (right) towards the campsites, and following it to the end. Alternatively the trails south of Adam Lake can be ridden from the Group Use Area, located further south of the campground along PTH 10.
Facilities: Camping, washrooms and water at Adam Lake Campground. Several huts and latrines along the trail system. Nearest full facilities at Boissevain.
Distance: Rides can be selected from over 50 km of trails as follows (note some trails overlap):

James Lake Trail (orange markers)	15 km
Adam Lake Trail (green)	10 km
Bower Lake Trail (yellow)	9 km
Intermediate Trail (blue)	5 km
John Lake Trail (green)	17 km
Vista Trail (orange)	5 km
Shoofly Trail (purple)	3 km

Difficulty: Easy to moderate (easy to difficult distances; moderate hills; easy surface).

Centered around Adam Lake is a dense network of trails, designated as either equestrian or hiking trails. This is one of the few instances where cycling on hiking and equestrian trails is recommended. However, these trails are more like broad, well maintained avenues, and there is ample space to accommodate both types of traffic. Check with parks about closures, and ride carefully. The number and variety of loops allow cyclists of just about every ability level to get out and enjoy.

As with the western segment of the park, there are multitudes of hills, and the trails have a grassy, easy-rolling surface. The exceptions are the newly cleared ones, particularly the James Lake and John Lake Trails. On these trails, watch for stumps and sheared shrubs which can grab your wheels, and for loose twigs which can break your derailleur. With time these trails will join the repertoire of well-surfaced rides. A beautiful new cabin for overnight accommodation presides over James Lake; advance registration is required from the Adam Lake Park Office.

From the parking area at the Adam Lake Campground a broad grassy area starts downhill: turn west (right) at the junction. The trail immediately zooms downhill, curving past the campground to another junction. Continue straight (north) if you want to ride the Intermediate Trail (blue), the Bower Lake Trail (yellow), or the James Lake Trail (orange). If the Adam Lake Trail (green) is your choice, or you want to head to the southern equestrian trails, turn west (left).

The Bower Lake Trail is representative of much of the trail system around Adam Lake. A wide, hard-packed surface gallops up and down moderate hills. Enjoy good views of Bower and other smaller lakes along the way. The forest is typically dense and filled with ash, Manitoba maples, birches, hazelnut, oak and aspen. Halfway along the trail is a well-maintained hut and latrine. The trail veers south, transforming into a long, gliding descent through a fabulous avenue of huge poplars. At the next junction select additional kilometers of the James Lake Trail (orange) to the west (right), or continue straight south and circle back to the campground along either the north shore or south shore of Adam Lake (the latter by connecting with the longer Adam Lake Trail). The trail south of Adam Lake has a delightful series of roller-coaster hills with a few views of the lake. Along the east end of Adam Lake the trail follows the highway ditch, dipping periodically into the forest. The trail emerges by the beach. Cross the causeway and follow the fitness trail to the right up the steep climb to the campsite.

When riding the southern equestrian trails, yield the right of way to horses. Hoof traffic has not affected the surface, although the John Lake Trail is rough from recent clearing. In combination with the James Lake Trail, explore over 25 km of solid, hilly riding, following the well signposted routes. These trails connect to the western roads and trails. Continue west from the southwest corner of the John Lake Trail along the park boundary to the junction of the Oskar Lake Road and the Boundary Road Trail (this connection has not been confirmed by bicycle).

The easiest ride in Turtle Mountain Park is to leave the parking lot at the campground, turn left at the trail junction and screech down the big hills to the lake. Be careful of walkers and runners. Traverse the causeway to the Group Use Area, and return to the main campground on the road. Whatever trail you select in Turtle Mountain Provincial Park, a rewarding and enjoyable ride is guaranteed.

Whiteshell Provincial Park

Whiteshell Provincial Park snuggles up against the Ontario border in eastern Manitoba. It ranks as the province's oldest and largest park, and is a popular outdoor playground. The Canadian Shield dominates the landscape, and much of the park is either very rocky or very wet. Mountain biking opportunities are fewer than the park's size might suggest, but the available trails span the full range of off road possibilities. Add variety to a vacation in the park, which might also include paved road cycling (p.73). For cottage owners, off road riding provides another means to explore the beauty of the Whiteshell throughout the cycling season.

The trails are clustered in the northeast, central and southern portions of the park. The riding surfaces, distances and difficulty levels reflect the individual character of the trails. Scoot along smooth forestry roads, improve your mountain biking skills along the grassy All Terrain Cycle (ATC) trails, or try the test of technical riding along the Biathlon Ski Trails.

Off road cycling in the Whiteshell is also a story of where not to ride. Hiking trails proliferate in the park, but must be avoided. The trails are very popular, and are usually too narrow, steep, rocky and short to be well-suited for mountain biking. Walking these trails is usually faster and more enjoyable for everyone. Although an extensive network of cross country ski and snowmobile trails covers the park, many of these cross swamps and lakes, and are impassable in the summer.

Northern Whiteshell

Type: Off road day rides; back roads and trails.
Access: Two ATC trails are accessed from the Bannock Point Staging Area off PR 307. The turnoff is immediately north of the Pine Point Hiking Trail parking area, and is marked only by a sign to the east of the highway identifying a rehabilitation camp. Ride here from your cottage or campsite, park at Pine Point parking area, or drive this access road to the actual staging area. Follow the gravel road, veering to the northwest (left) at the Y-junction before crossing the river. Immediately at the top of the riverbank is a grassy parking area to the east (left). A third ATC trail leaves from the south side of PR 309 near Big Whiteshell. No designated parking area.
Facilities: None at trailhead or along trails. Drinking water and latrines at

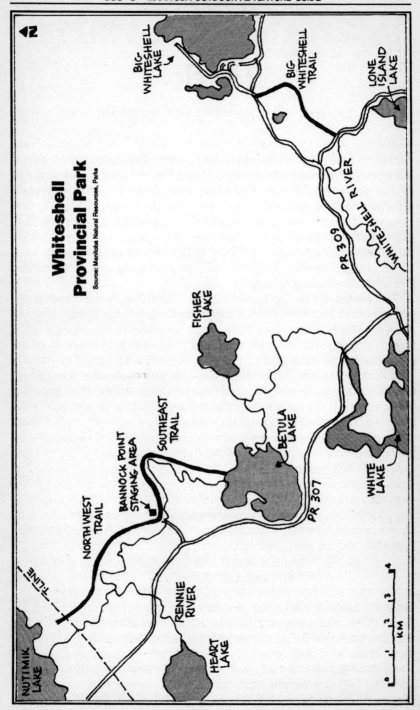

Whiteshell Provincial Park

Source: Manitoba Natural Resources, Parks

Pine Point parking area. Nearest full facilities at Betula Lake, Nutimik Lake or Big Whiteshell Lake.

Distances: The ATC trails are estimated as follows:

Northwest trail	5 km one way
Southeast trail	6 km one way
Big Whiteshell Trail	4 km one way

Difficulty: Easy (easy distances and hills; easy to moderate surface).

From Bannock Point diverge two short and pleasant rides. Both are designated ATC trails, but offer different riding surfaces and experiences. One is an old road, guaranteeing smooth, easy pedaling. The second is a grassy trail with higher rolling resistance, but gentle hills and a lakeside destination. Both are good family riding trails.

To reach the northwest trail, ride further north from the Bannock Point parking area. At the junction with the yellow ATC trail sign, turn northwest (left; the road straight ahead is closed to all vehicle traffic including bicycles). Cruise this wide, level road past rows of aspen, ash and the occasional spruce. The trail parallels the Whiteshell River but glimpses of water are few. Zip past a walleye pond, then pump up a few curving hills to the end of the trail. It ends abruptly at a transmission line and a jumble of rocks, and you must return by the same route. This road is muddy after heavy rains.

The southeast ATC trail leads off into dense deciduous forest from the southeast (right hand) corner of the parking area. The trail doubles as a snowmobile trail, and is considerably narrower and rougher than the previous one. A lush cover of grass hides unexpected dips and wet areas, but this is not an arduous trail. It rises gently as it swings round the bend of the Whiteshell River, then emerges on the shores of Betula Lake. Return to the parking area by the same route. If you don't like the biting flies of the Whiteshell, avoid this trail in mid-summer.

Another ATC trail leads off PR 309 and swings in an arc near Big Whiteshell Lake. Although it has not been checked by bicycle, the trail has good riding potential, with moderate hills, gravel pits, and few wetlands. The trail leads to the Lone Island Lake Road. You could swing back on the highway or return by the same route. Several other ridable trails are rumored to be in the vicinity.

Central Whiteshell

Type: Off road day rides; roads and trails.
Access: Two trails depart from Inverness Falls Road at the northern end of Brereton Lake, off PR 307. Follow the gravel road briefly, taking the first turn to the north (right). Park anywhere off the road.
Facilities: Water at trail head; none along trail. Nearest full facilities at Inverness Falls or Brereton Lake.
Distance: The shortest ride on the Rice Lake trails is less than 10 km; the

Central Whiteshell

Source: Manitoba Natural Resources, Parks

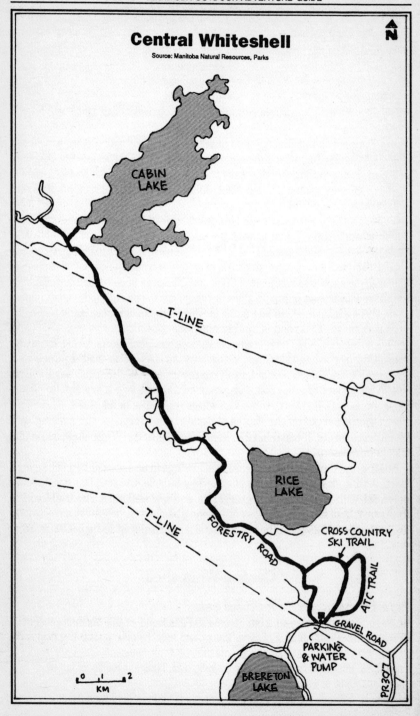

N

CABIN LAKE

T-LINE

T-LINE

RICE LAKE

FORESTRY ROAD

CROSS COUNTRY SKI TRAIL

ATC TRAIL

GRAVEL ROAD

PARKING & WATER PUMP

PR 307

BRERETON LAKE

0 1 2
KM

trip to Cabin Lake along the forestry roads is approximately 18 km return.
Difficulty: Moderate (easy to difficult distances; moderate hills; easy to moderate surface).

The two trails near Inverness Falls contrast in distance, difficulty, and riding surface. The shorter ATC trail follows grassy ski trails and requires slower, more technical riding. Spin quickly and easily along a network of forestry roads, eating up the kilometers to Cabin Lake or further destinations.

The ATC trail leads north of the staging area, marked by the yellow sign. It describes a stretched circle beside and partly following cross country ski trails. Limited signs confuse navigation and the directions below are approximate. Follow the ATC trail, veering right at the first junction. These first few kilometers are the most rugged, with hidden ruts and rocks to grab your wheels. Sand and jack pines appear near a shelter and a map of the ski trails. Keeping the shelter to your left, ride past it, then select the trail (an old road) to the west (left). Spin easily as the road swings south, although sandy patches slow you down. Ignore a left turn at the next junction in a small sand pit, and continue straight to the forestry road. Turn southeast (left) to return to the parking area along the forestry road.

The forestry road heads to the northwest from the parking area (to the left of the ATC trail). Active logging is underway, so temper any midweek skimming with a healthy respect for speeding logging trucks. The road begins with a few curving climbs through aspen, maple, ash and jack pine. Pass a less-traveled turn to the south (left) which leads towards Inverness Falls, and pass the junction of the ATC/ski trail to the north (right). Settle into the pattern of twists and turns, gradual uphills and freewheeling descents. Fly past shallow Rice Lake, in summer a dry depression to the right. Skim out of close deciduous forests into open rocky jack pine areas. Several roads branch to the southeast (left), leading to the Rennie River.

Follow the main road under two sets of transmission lines up onto a rocky area and to a Y-junction. Zip down the road to the east (right) and within a few turns of the crank you arrive at Cabin Lake. Swim and relax before returning by the same route. The road to the left, with a gate, branches extensively, inviting further exploration. These roads have not been checked by bicycle, but the more southern of the branches (to the left) which recrosses the transmission lines may extend furthest west. Much of this area has been clear-cut.

Adventuresome mountain bikers could try exploring some of the trails leading off to the east of PR 307. Be prepared for disappointment, as many of the trails which appear on the topographic map are overgrown or disappear into swamp. This is also true for several trail heads visible from the highway.

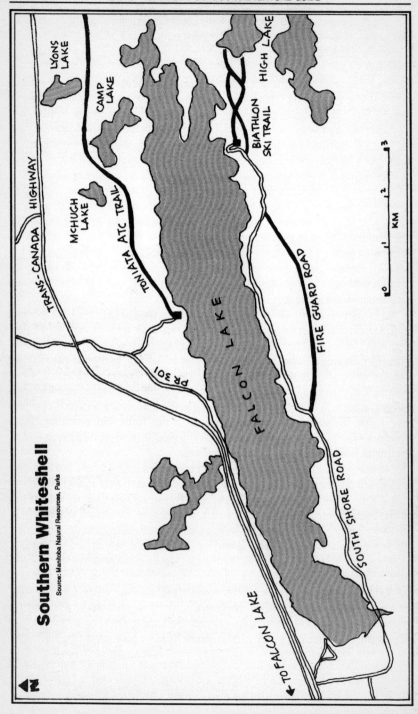

Southern Whiteshell

Source: Manitoba Natural Resources, Parks

LYONS LAKE

CAMP LAKE

McHUGH LAKE

HIGH LAKE

BIATHLON SKI TRAIL

TRANS-CANADA HIGHWAY

TONIATA ATC TRAIL

FALCON LAKE

FIRE GUARD ROAD

PR 301

SOUTH SHORE ROAD

TO FALCON LAKE

0 1 2 3
KM

N

Southern Whiteshell

Type: Off road day rides; back roads and trails.

Access: Trails center around Falcon Lake. Two accesses for the fire guard road lead from South Shore Road: the only two turnoffs heading south. Access to the Biathlon Ski Trail is at the end of South Drive, on the way to Falcon Lake Ski Resort. Park at the gate across the road. Access to the Toniata ATC Trail is on the road to Toniata off PR 301, marked by a large sign.

Facilities: None at any of the trail heads or along trails. Full facilities in Falcon Lake or Toniata.

Distances: Approximate distances as follows:

Fire guard road	6 km one way
Biathlon Trail	up to 10 km
Toniata ATC Trail	more than 8 km one way

Difficulty: Fire guard road and Toniata ATC trail: easy to moderate (distances, hills and surface); Biathlon Trail: difficult (hills and surface; moderate distances).

Consistent with the pattern of off road riding trails in the rest of the Whiteshell, the Falcon Lake area offers contrasting cycling options. Sail smoothly along the fire guard road, push through the grass and the swamps of the ATC Trail, or pick your way among the rocks and trees of the Biathlon Trail.

The fire guard road is a hilly and smooth delight, running parallel to the main cottage road along the south shore of Falcon Lake. Combine it with the gravel cottage road for a rollicking 12 km circle ride from Falcon Lake town. In addition to the constant ups and downs, there is an overall climb to the east. Traffic is heavy on the cottage road during summer weekends.

For those intrigued by technical challenges, the Biathlon Trail at Falcon offers them in abundance. Wedged between the downhill ski slopes and High Lake, a network of trails maximizes the vertical gain offered by the Canadian Shield rock. The same rock demands tricky and agile hopping to negotiate. Many of the trails are recently cleared, and stumps grab your front tires. The reward at the end is beautiful High Lake.

From the gate on the South Shore Drive, cruise the initial kilometers along the smooth road. Take the first turn to the right to swing up to the top of the ski hills. Enjoy the view, then scream down the east slope into the woods and follow the road to the east (left), swinging right to grunt up the next hill. Follow the trail to the T-junction. Turn northeast (left), ignoring the orange hiker sign pointing right (this leads to the wetter High Lake Hiking Trail). Now the rough stuff begins. Follow the newly cut trail up and down the hillside. Glance up from the rocks and stumps to admire the aspen and spruce forests. Slowly descend the makeshift bridge of logs and straw, and continue inching your way along the hillside, gradually climbing. This trail rejoins a more traveled route. Follow t briefly, looking carefully for the turnoff to the left which immediately swings sharply to the right, negotiating trees and a large rock. The trail is now a hiking path, crossing logs and skirting rocks. Walk the bikes down a steep ravine and across the trickle, climb to the crest, and then follow the path to High Lake. To return, follow the trail out to the main path, turn west (right) and ride to the first clear right turn. This trail can be wet and muddy, as it follows the bottom of a rock ridge back to the foot of the ski slopes. Cut diagonally up and across the downhill runs to rejoin the road back to the cars.

The Toniata ATC Trail runs north of Falcon Lake along the pipeline. Although not checked by bicycle, navigation is easy: stick to the pipeline. Several ski trails intersect, but most of these lead to lakes or marshes. The trail is reportedly grassy, over gently rolling hills with the odd steep one. Some wetlands may bog down cyclists, but the worst area is apparently close to the trail head. This trail may not be ridable in the spring or during a wet summer. Ride as far as you want or the terrain allows: the trail continues into Ontario and parts east.

Ruth Marr

Index